Simple Comforts

MARY BERRY

Simple Comforts

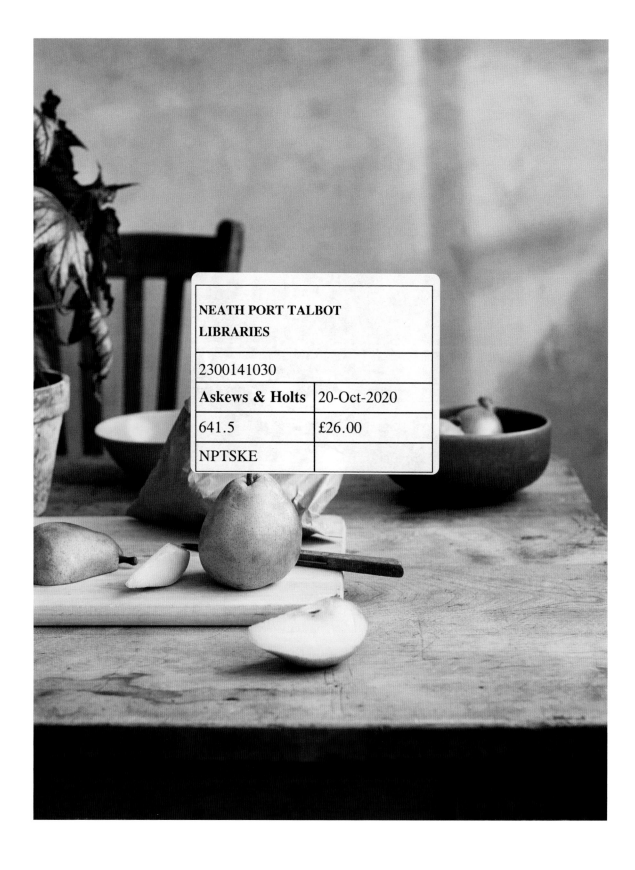

Contents

INTRODUCTION 7

COOK'S NOTES 12

MARY'S RECIPE FINDER 15

Sharing & First Courses 21

Poultry & Game 47

Fish & Seafood 81

Pork, Beef & Lamb 109

Vegetable Mains 151

Salads & Sides 181

Puddings 219

Bakes 255

Mary's Kitchen Guidance 283

INDEX 295

ACKNOWLEDGEMENTS 302

Introduction

Good food is one of the great joys of life. Cooking a superb meal is a wonderful way of expressing love and giving comfort and pleasure to family and friends. And you don't have to be a three-star chef. Comfort food should be easy to make and I like dishes that can be put together reasonably quickly without stress or too many ingredients. I've done my best to make the recipes in this book as straightforward as possible.

The very words 'comfort food' are like a big warm hug for most of us. Comfort food means different things to different people. For many, it will be a roast Sunday dinner that says family and togetherness. For others, it may be a perfect tomato salad that gives you the feeling of being in a sunlit Mediterranean café, or a home-made cake that fills the house with tempting aromas as it bakes in the oven. You may associate comfort dishes with guilty pleasures such as chips and chocolate, but I believe that good food can be both comforting and perfectly healthy. Think of classic soups, for example, which are always so cheering. Try something hearty and warming in the colder months, such as the Warming Chicken Noodle Soup on page 24 or the delightfully colourful Marigold Soup on page 22, made with lovely winter root vegetables; comforting, nourishing and easy to make – what more can you ask? And in spring, try my Emerald Isle Garden Soup (page 29), which looks as good as it tastes and can be enjoyed hot or cold.

Food is for sharing and one of my favourite treats to share as a first course or a light lunch is burrata – that wonderfully indulgent Italian cheese. Have a look at my recipe on page 42 for Burrata with Heritage Tomato Salad. This couldn't be easier to put together and has an unusual Bloody Mary dressing to make it extra special. Wraps are another great sharing dish and I love the Mexican Chicken and Avocado Sharing Platter on page 59 and the Mixed Bean and Butternut Wraps on page 171. There's a recipe for making wraps if you like, or you can buy them if you're short of time.

Perhaps the ultimate comfort meal for many of us is a roast chicken. Just the thought brings a smile to my face. My family loves it with all the trimmings in autumn and winter, or served with some beautiful salads on a summer day. A plain roast chicken is completely delicious but try my latest version on page 50. You simply mix some butter with flavourings such as ginger, tarragon and lemon zest and spread it under the skin of the breast. Simple to do and then you just pop the chicken in the oven and wait for a feast!

I know chicken dishes are a great favourite in many families, so I've included plenty of recipes here, such as Chicken Hot Pot with Potato Topping (page 52) which is hearty and healthy and perfect for supper with friends. Sausages in any form are among the most comforting of all foods and I think you will find the Spicy Sausage Rolls (page 110) meet with everyone's approval. While I often like to make quick dishes for supper, such as the Stir-fried Chicken and Vegetable Rice on page 68, at weekends I find that slow-cooked dishes fit the bill. You can pop something such as the French Slow-roast Lamb with Ratatouille (page 144) or Boeuf Bourguignon (page 138) in the oven and leave it to cook gently while you relax or enjoy a walk. You come back to a kitchen filled with savoury aromas and a splendid meal with the minimum of effort.

Another aspect of comfort food is the memories it evokes. My husband spent some of his life in Sri Lanka and always enjoys food that reminds him of those days, such as my Sri Lankan Chicken Curry (page 60). It's easy to make and full of great flavour. And for me, a simple dish of trout takes me back to the days when our children were young, and we used to go fishing. One of the first fish our son Thomas caught, at ten years old, was a sea trout, and a favourite fish dish in our house is Whole Stuffed Baked Trout with Caper Butter (page 100).

Some people are nervous about cooking fish, but in this book you'll find plenty of fish dishes that are very easy to make. Try the Cod Goujons with Caper Herb Dip on page 105 and serve it with sweet potato chips for a healthy version of that favourite comfort dish fish and chips, or Salmon Fillets with Cauliflower Cheese Topping (page 102) for a simple supper that's full of flavour. Pasta is a great favourite in our house and Crab Linguine (page 82) is ready in the time it takes to boil the pasta.

I know that for many people baking is therapeutic and cheering. I am one of them! Whipping up a cake, a loaf of bread or some biscuits can lift the spirits no end – even before you eat the results. In this book you will find some real treasures, from Focaccia with Olives, Tomatoes and Rosemary (page 281) to divine chocolate cakes and a version of my all-time favourite biscuit – Orange Shortbread Fingers (page 263). And, of course, there are plenty of puddings ranging from those ultimate comfort desserts Apple and Blackberry Crumble (page 248) and a very special Bread and Butter Pudding (page 242) to a simple Lemon and Blueberry Mousse (page 228) and the decadent Irish Cream and Cherry Pots (page 231).

Particularly when I'm entertaining guests or expecting the family around, I like to make life easier by getting as much done as I can ahead of time. That way I can concentrate on people rather than getting stuck in the kitchen. For most of the recipes in this book I've given advice on what elements you can prepare ahead. Some dishes are even better when made the day before eating! I've also added tips of what can be cooked and stored in the freezer until needed – very useful for busy times like Christmas or other celebrations. Dishes such as Mexican Chilli Con Carne (page 135) and Cottage Pie (page 136) can be made the day before you want to eat them and the Smoky Beef Casserole with Black-Eyed Beans on page 130 can be made up to two days ahead. I often like to get going with desserts early in the day when I'm entertaining, particularly if I'm cooking a main course that needs last-minute attention. In the pudding chapter you will find cold desserts such as Wild Bramble Mousse (page 227) that can be made the day before, and others such as a wonderfully indulgent Brioche Frangipane Apple Pudding (page 240) that can be cooked in the morning and then reheated and whipped out of the oven to delight your guests.

As always, I've kept the recipes as clear and concise as possible and in this book, we have a glorious photograph of every dish to inspire you. I know that it is always helpful to have a picture to aspire to. I've loved putting this collection of simple, comforting recipes together and I hope you get as much pleasure from them as I do.

Mary Berry

Cook's notes

When you're using the recipes in this book, you're welcome to make little tweaks of your own. While it's best to follow exact weights where these are given first time round, next time you make the recipes, you might like to use a bit more or a bit less of something to suit your taste. Equally, you might prefer to substitute one type of cheese for another in a recipe or use a different kind of fish or meat. Feel free to experiment.

- Both metric and imperial measures are provided. When you're weighing out ingredients, it's best to go by one or the other – never mix the two. (See also the Conversion Tables on pages 288–89.) Spoon measures are level unless otherwise stated.

- In recipes for cakes and other baked items, the ingredients need to be measured carefully. I find that digital scales are best for the purpose.

- For oven temperatures, the standard Centigrade measure is given first, followed by the fan temperature, 20 degrees less in each case. (See also the Conversion Tables on pages 288–89.) As ovens vary in the amount of heat they produce, you may need to cook a dish for slightly more or less time, depending on your own particular oven. It can be helpful to use an oven thermometer to gauge the correct temperature for cooking a dish.

- Try to buy the best-quality meat and fish that you can afford – free range, in the case of meat, and sustainably sourced fish. Check with your fishmonger, or at the fish counter in your local supermarket, and use an alternative type of fish if you find that the kind you have selected is no longer on the sustainability list – which changes according to fish stock levels.

- Where a type of cooking oil isn't specified, use any oil that you like, although it's best to choose something relatively mild, such as sunflower oil, that won't overpower the flavour of the dish. For dressings, use the best-quality oil that you can afford, to give the most intense flavour.

- Use large eggs, unless otherwise stated – free range, if possible. If you are vegetarian, you might prefer to use suitable cheeses that don't contain animal rennet.

- I use granulated sugar for general sweetening; caster sugar, which is finer, for baking; and icing sugar for icing. Light muscovado gives a great flavour and demerara creates delicious crunchy toppings and adds a fudgy flavour to cakes and puddings. All these sugars keep for long periods in sealed containers. If you find sugar becomes a solid block in the bag, store a clean, damp J-cloth in the bag to separate the grains.

- Modern milling techniques mean that it is not always necessary to sift flour. I always specify in a recipe where it is needed.

- To turn plain flour into self-raising flour, add 2–3 teaspoons of baking powder to every 200g (7oz) of plain flour. Check the sell-by dates on flour and baking powder.

Mary's recipe finder

We've arranged all the dishes in this book into a number of different categories to help you find the recipe you need. Whether you are looking for a tasty soup, a quick supper, something that you can prepare ahead or a delicious feast for a crowd, I hope you will find just the dish you want in the following pages.

SOUPS

Marigold soup 22

Warming chicken noodle soup 24

Mushroom & leek soup 26

Emerald Isle garden soup 29

SIMPLE STARTERS

Double-baked mushroom soufflés 30

Rustic smoked trout & anchovy pâté 33

Pea & mint dip 38

LIGHT LUNCHES & SHARING PLATES

Spinach frittata quiche 34

Stuffed portabella mushrooms with
  Brie & spinach 36

Croque Monsieur 41

Burrata with heritage tomato salad
  & Bloody Mary dressing 42

Mixed bean & butternut wraps 171

Toasted muffins with scrambled eggs
  & smoked salmon 44

Crab & herb blinis with pickled fennel salad 84

Warm chicken Caesar, bacon & avocado wraps 62

Open chicken, bacon & avocado sandwich
  with maple dressing 64

SALADS

Orzo salad with grilled vegetables & olives 156

Greek salad with feta & olive tapenade 210

Roasted pepper & tomato salad with broad beans 212

Rosy-pink beetroot, feta & olive salad 215

Roasted pepper, mushroom & broccoli brown
  rice salad 216

Hot smoked salmon & asparagus salad 87

Warm chicken & dill salad with mustard
  Parmesan dressing 72

Duck salad with hoisin dressing 75

MAKE-AHEAD MEALS

Veggie burgers 152

Preserved lemon chicken 48

Sri Lankan chicken curry 60

Chicken & fennel fricassee with tarragon 70

Pheasant & port stew 76

Smoky beef casserole with black-eyed beans 130

Cottage pie with a bit of a kick 136

Boeuf Bourguignon 138

Mexican chilli con carne 135

Swedish meatballs with enriched apple
  & thyme sauce 114

SPEEDY SUPPERS

Paneer & roasted vegetable curry 168

Super veg with brown rice & herbs 178

Grilled garlic prawns & Mediterranean vegetables 88

Whole stuffed baked trout with caper butter 100

Salmon fillets with cauliflower cheese topping 102

Cod goujons with caper herb dip 105

Stir-fried chicken & vegetable rice 68

Mustard kidneys 148

ONE-POT DISHES

Roasting tin Thai salmon & vegetables 92

Salmon & fennel one-pot wonder 94

Haddock & shrimp feast 96

Chicken hot pot with potato topping 52

Sausage & red pepper hot pot 117

PASTA

Penne pasta with peppers, garlic mushrooms
 & asparagus 159

Mac 'n' cheese 154

Crab linguine 82

Baked pasta lasagne rolls 112

Posh bacon, asparagus & mushroom spaghetti 121

Bolognese bake 128

PASTRY

Sweet potato & spinach pithivier 164

Onion, artichoke & sage open tart 166

Leek & dill quiche with a choice of toppings 176

Pork en croute with Stilton & apple 124

Matchday beef & ale shortcrust pie 140

Spicy sausage rolls 110

WEEKEND SPECIALS

Golden cauliflower steaks with tomato
 & garlic salsa 163

Cauliflower, broccoli & leek Mornay 175

Thai cod cakes with Thai basil & lime sauce 99

Seafood risotto 91

Glorious fish pie 106

Roast chicken with tarragon butter & melting onions 50

Mild curried chicken with grapes & asparagus 55

Spiced quail with coriander dressing 78

Marinated harissa & yoghurt pork kebabs 118

Mustard steak with vine tomatoes & foolproof
 Béarnaise sauce 132

French slow-roast lamb with ratatouille 144

Rack of lamb with garlic minted potatoes 147

FEEDING A CROWD

Mushroom, lentil & double potato jumble 160

Posh jacket potatoes 172

Five-spiced chicken with coriander & cucumber relish 56

Mexican chicken & avocado sharing platter 59

Smoky firecracker chicken drumsticks 67

Slow-roast hand & spring with crackling
 & onion gravy 122

Orange-glazed ham with mango & orange salsa 126

Braised lamb with sweet potato & haricot beans 143

ACCOMPANIMENTS

Squash & parsnip roasties 182

Fragrant lemongrass & coriander rice 184

Ridged garlic potatoes 186

Colcannon mash 189

The best roast potatoes 190

Yorkshire pudding 193

Potato wedges with soured cream chive dip 194

Split roasted butternut squash with chilli
   garlic butter 196

Carrot & swede purée 198

Sweet potato skinny fries 201

Pickled beetroot 202

Golden roasted vegetables 204

Simmered red cabbage & cider 206

Stir-fried aromatic Hispi cabbage 209

COLD PUDDINGS

Celebration trifle 220

Lemon posset tart with fresh raspberries 222

Divine white chocolate chilled cheesecake 224

Wild bramble mousse 227

Lemon & blueberry mousse with hazelnut
   & oat topping 228

Irish Cream & cherry pots 231

Chocolate & raspberry layered pots 232

Lemon ripple ice cream 234

Decadent orange, chocolate & whisky mousse 237

HOT PUDDINGS

Warming autumn fruit compote 238

Brioche frangipane apple pudding 240

Bread & butter pudding with pecan maple
   topping 242

Toffee pear pudding 245

Chocolate steamed pudding with chocolate sauce 246

Apple & blackberry crumble 248

Rustic apple tart 250

SMALL CAKES & BISCUITS

Bakewell tart fingers 256

Lemon shortbread with raspberries & cream 258

Cranberry, orange & pistachio biscuits 260

Orange shortbread fingers 263

Tiny chocolate cupcakes 264

LARGE CAKES

Chocolate & strawberry dessert cake 267

Chocolate yoghurt cake 268

Coffee & hazelnut praline cake 270

Granny's gingerbread 273

Passion fruit lemon cake 274

Tea loaf with cranberries & sultanas 276

BREAD

Irish soda bread 278

Focaccia with olives, tomatoes & rosemary 281

Sharing &
First Courses

Marigold soup

This soup is a beautiful bright orange colour – like the flower – and is so
warming and cheering in the winter months, when root vegetables are at their best.
Some of the cooked vegetables are puréed and some not, which brings
an interesting texture to the soup.

SERVES 6

25g (1oz) butter
2 onions, thinly sliced
250g (9oz) butternut squash,
 peeled and finely diced
250g (9oz) swede, peeled and
 finely diced
350g (12oz) carrots, peeled and
 finely diced
1.2 litres (2 pints) chicken or
 vegetable stock
25g (1oz) pumpkin seeds,
 toasted
1 tbsp chopped parsley
Salt and freshly ground black
 pepper

PREPARE AHEAD
Can be made up to 2 days ahead.

FREEZE
Freezes well.

1 Melt the butter in a large, deep saucepan. Add the vegetables and
 fry them over a high heat for 5 minutes. Pour in the stock. Season
 with salt and pepper, cover the pan and bring the soup to the boil.
 Reduce the heat and simmer over a low heat for about 15 minutes
 or until all the vegetables are tender.

2 Using a slotted spoon, scoop out about a third of the cooked
 vegetables. Blend these, either with a hand blender or in a free-
 standing blender or food processor, until smooth. Pour the
 mixture back into the soup, stir and check the seasoning.

3 Serve hot, and sprinkle each bowlful with pumpkin seeds and
 chopped parsley.

Warming chicken noodle soup

Hearty and comforting, this is the ultimate main meal soup.
It's full of flavour and will be loved by all.

SERVES 6

1.75 litres (3 pints) good chicken
   stock
450g (1lb) skinless and boneless
   chicken thigh fillets
6 thyme sprigs
25g (1oz) butter
1 small leek, thinly sliced
1 onion, thinly sliced
1 thin carrot, peeled and thinly
   sliced into rounds
1 small garlic clove, crushed
150g (5oz) button mushrooms,
   sliced
130g (4½oz) medium egg
   noodles
2 tbsp chopped parsley
Salt and freshly ground black
   pepper

1   Heat the chicken stock in a saucepan over a high heat. Add the
    chicken thighs and thyme and bring to a rolling boil. Lower the
    heat and leave to simmer gently for about 25 minutes until the
    chicken is cooked through and tender. Remove the chicken with
    a slotted spoon and slice it or pull apart into thin strips. Set the
    stock aside.

2   Melt the butter in another large pan. Add the leek, onion and
    carrot and fry over a high heat for about 3-4 minutes. Add the
    garlic and fry for 30 seconds. Strain in the hot stock and bring
    to the boil, then add the mushrooms and simmer for about
    10 minutes.

3   Cook the noodles in a pan of boiling water according to the
    packet instructions. Drain, then run under cold water.

4   Add the chicken and noodles to the soup and heat them through.
    Check the seasoning and serve sprinkled with parsley.

Mushroom & leek soup

So simple to make, this is a good soup and warming to the heart. It's my favourite lunchtime meal and I enjoy it all year round. Choose a variety of white mushrooms, such as button, closed cup and even chestnut.

SERVES 4–6

1 tbsp sunflower oil

A knob of butter

350g (12oz) white mushrooms, sliced

3 leeks, sliced

2 large potatoes, peeled and cut into small dice

750ml (1 pint 6fl oz) chicken or vegetable stock

4 tbsp pouring double cream

1 tbsp finely chopped tarragon

Salt and freshly ground black pepper

PREPARE AHEAD
Can be made up to 2 days ahead.

FREEZE
Freezes well.

1 Heat the oil and butter in a saucepan. Add the mushrooms and leeks and fry for 3 minutes. Cover with a lid for 1 minute, then remove the lid and fry for another minute.

2 Add the diced potatoes and stock. Cover the pan and simmer gently over a low heat for about 15 minutes or until the potatoes are tender.

3 Blend until smooth, either with a hand blender or in a freestanding blender or food processor. Season, then add the cream and tarragon to serve.

Emerald Isle garden soup

Named for its bright green colour, this soup is wonderfully healthy and hearty and is delicious hot or cold. The brief cooking time helps keep the vibrant colour, and adding some extra little florets of broccoli at the end gives texture. If the soup seems a little on the thick side, slacken it with some extra stock.

SERVES 4–6

350g (12oz) head of broccoli
1 tbsp sunflower oil
A knob of butter
3 leeks, sliced
1 green pepper, deseeded and finely diced
2 large courgettes, diced
1 garlic clove, crushed
900ml (1½ pints) chicken or vegetable stock, plus extra if needed
225g (8oz) frozen petits pois, defrosted
Salt and freshly ground black pepper
Pouring double cream, to serve (optional)

PREPARE AHEAD
Can be made up to 2 days ahead and served hot or cold.

FREEZE
Freezes well.

1 Remove the stalk of the broccoli. Peel off the tough outer skin, then finely dice the stalk. Split the broccoli into large florets, then slice into tiny ones. Reserve a small pile of florets for later.

2 Heat a wide-based saucepan and add the oil and butter. When they are foaming, add the leeks and fry for 2 minutes. Add the pepper, courgettes, broccoli stalk and garlic and fry for 2–3 minutes over a medium heat, stirring. Pour in most of the stock, reserving about 100ml (3½fl oz), and season with salt and pepper. Cover and simmer for about 5 minutes. Add the peas and broccoli florets and cook for a further 4 minutes until tender.

3 Blend the soup, either with a hand blender or in a free-standing blender or food processor, until completely smooth, adding the remaining stock if necessary.

4 Bring the soup to the boil and add the reserved tiny broccoli florets. Boil for 2 minutes to cook the florets and serve piping hot in bowls, with a little swirl of cream, if using, and some crusty bread on the side.

Double-baked mushroom soufflés

Pure indulgence in the best way! You can make these simple mushroom and cheese soufflés well ahead of time, then reheat them in the creamy spinach sauce and they still stand tall.

SERVES 6

75g (3oz) butter, plus extra
   for greasing
200g (7oz) chestnut mushrooms,
   finely diced
50g (2oz) plain flour
300ml (10fl oz) hot full-fat milk
3 eggs, separated
50g (2oz) Gruyère cheese, grated
50g (2oz) Parmesan cheese,
   grated
Salt and freshly ground black
   pepper

FOR THE SAUCE
300ml (10fl oz) pouring double
   cream
50g (2oz) baby spinach, roughly
   chopped
2 tsp Dijon mustard

PREPARE AHEAD
*Can be made up to 8 hours
ahead and reheated with the
sauce as in step 8.*

1   You will need 6 x size 1 (100ml) ramekins. Preheat the oven to 220°C/200°C fan/Gas 7 and butter the ramekins generously. Lay a piece of kitchen paper in the base of a roasting tin – the paper stops the ramekins slipping in the tin.

2   Melt 25g (1oz) of the butter in a large, non-stick frying pan, add the mushrooms and fry them over a high heat for a few minutes. Cover the pan with a lid, lower the heat and cook for another 4 minutes, then remove the lid and fry over a high heat to evaporate the liquid. Remove the mushrooms with a slotted spoon and set them aside.

3   To make the soufflé base, melt the remaining butter in a saucepan. Whisk in the flour to make a roux and cook for a minute. Gradually add the hot milk and whisk over a high heat until you have a thickened, smooth sauce.

4   Remove the pan from the heat and beat in the egg yolks, one at a time, until the sauce is smooth. Add the mushrooms and the cheese and season, then set aside to cool a little.

5   Whisk the egg whites until soft peaks form. Stir about a tablespoon of egg whites into the egg and mushroom mixture and carefully fold it in, keeping everything light and airy.

6   Divide the soufflé mixture evenly between the ramekins and sit them on the paper in the roasting tin. Pour enough boiling water into the tin to come halfway up the sides of the ramekins. Bake the soufflés for about 15 minutes until risen and lightly golden.

7   To make the sauce, pour the cream into a jug and add the spinach and mustard. Season with salt and pepper and stir to combine.

8   To serve, preheat the oven to 220°C/200°C fan/Gas 7. Carefully run a knife around the edge of each ramekin and remove the soufflés. Sit the soufflés, browned side up, in an ovenproof dish, then spoon the sauce around them. Reheat for about 12 minutes until piping hot. Serve with dressed leaves or some brown bread.

Rustic smoked trout & anchovy pâté

Pâté is so comforting and makes such a generous sharing dish. Quick and easy to prepare, this pâté is delicious served with hot toast and makes a lovely starter or a great weekend lunch served with pickled beetroot (see page 202). Take care to keep some texture in the mixture – it shouldn't be a smooth purée. Packets of smoked trout fillets are available in most supermarkets and the fillets look similar to poached salmon.

SERVES 4

50g (2oz) butter, softened
2 anchovy fillets, roughly
    chopped
3 tbsp chopped dill, plus extra
    to garnish
1 tbsp hot horseradish sauce
100g (4oz) full-fat crème fraîche
125g (4½ oz) smoked rainbow
    trout fillets
Juice of ½ small lemon
1 tbsp chopped capers
Salt and freshly ground black
    pepper

TO SERVE
Sourdough bread

PREPARE AHEAD
*Can be made up to a day ahead
and kept in the fridge, then served
at room temperature.*

1   Measure the softened butter and anchovies into a small bowl and mash them together with a fork.

2   Spoon the mixture into a food processor, then add the dill, horseradish and crème fraîche. Season with a little salt and pepper, then whizz quickly for a few seconds. Add the trout fillets, lemon juice and capers and whizz again for a few seconds until just mixed but still with some texture. Check the seasoning, then spoon the mixture into a small rustic bowl.

3   Toast the bread and serve the pâté garnished with dill and with some pickled beetroot on the side.

Spinach frittata quiche

Our family loves a frittata and we also love quiche, but we don't always want pastry. This is a combination of the two and we think it is a real treat. It makes a great sharing plate too.

SERVES 4–6

A knob of butter, for greasing
4 rashers of thick-cut smoked bacon, chopped
100g (4oz) baby spinach
8 large eggs
150ml (5fl oz) pouring double cream
175g (6oz) Gruyère cheese, grated
Salt and freshly ground black pepper

PREPARE AHEAD
Can be made up to 8 hours ahead and served cold.

1 You will need a fixed-base 20cm (8in) cake tin with deep sides. Preheat the oven to 180°C/160°C fan/Gas 4. Grease the sides of the tin thoroughly with butter and line the base with a disc of baking paper.

2 Heat a frying pan over a high heat and fry the bacon until crisp. Remove with a slotted spoon and set aside. Add the spinach and fry until it has just wilted, then drain and squeeze out the liquid. Roughly chop and set aside.

3 Whisk the eggs and cream together in a large bowl. Add the bacon, spinach and cheese, then season well and pour into the prepared tin. Bake for 30 minutes until firm around the edges and just set in the middle.

4 Leave to cool slightly before turning out from the tin. You might need to run a palette knife round the edge before releasing the quiche from the tin. Turn out carefully on to a tea towel covering a plate, then reverse it on to another plate. Serve warm in wedges, with a dressed salad.

Stuffed portabella mushrooms, with Brie & spinach

Quick to prepare, this is a perfect dish to serve as a starter, light lunch or as part of a summer buffet. Choose fat, deep portabella mushrooms rather than thin ones, as the fat ones stand prouder.

SERVES 4

2 tbsp olive oil
A knob of butter
4 large fat portabella mushrooms, stalks removed
2 large red onions, sliced
1 tbsp balsamic glaze
100g (4oz) Brie, sliced into 4 pieces
200g (7oz) baby spinach
4 slices of Parma ham
Salt and freshly ground black pepper

PREPARE AHEAD
Can be assembled up to 4 hours ahead, ready for the oven.

1 Preheat the oven to 200°C/180°C fan/Gas 6. Line a baking sheet with baking paper or non-stick paper.

2 Heat a tablespoon of the oil with the butter in a large frying pan. Add the mushrooms, gill side up, and fry for a few minutes. Cover the pan with a lid and fry for another 4 minutes. Remove the lid, turn the mushrooms over and fry them for a minute or two until all the liquid has evaporated. Sit the mushrooms, gill side up, on the baking sheet and season with salt and pepper.

3 Add the remaining tablespoon of oil to the pan and fry the onions for about 5–8 minutes until just soft. Stir in the balsamic, then spoon the onions on top of the mushrooms and place a piece of Brie on each one.

4 Add the spinach to the pan, season with salt and pepper, then stir for a few minutes until just wilted. Spoon the spinach on top of the cheese and sit a swirl of Parma ham on top.

5 Bake for about 8–10 minutes until the ham is crispy and the mushrooms are tender. If liquid comes out on to the baking sheet, remove from the oven and carefully drain it off.

6 Serve hot, with a dressed salad.

Pea & mint dip

This dip works well served with breadsticks, flatbreads or sticks of raw vegetables, or spread on toast and topped with smoked mackerel fillets. It's fine to use low-fat mayonnaise and crème fraîche for this recipe if you prefer.

MAKES A SMALL BOWLFUL

150g (5oz) frozen petits pois
400g (14oz) tin of chickpeas, drained
½ garlic clove, crushed
Juice of 1 small lemon
Small bunch of mint (about 15g/½oz), leaves chopped
2 tbsp mayonnaise
3 tbsp crème fraîche
Salt and freshly ground black pepper

PREPARE AHEAD
Can be made up to a day ahead.

1 Measure the petits pois into a pan of boiling salted water. Boil for 4 minutes, then drain. Run them under cold water, then drain again and place on kitchen paper to dry.

2 Spoon the chickpeas into a food processor and add the garlic, lemon juice, mint, mayonnaise, crème fraîche and the cooked peas. Season with salt and pepper, then whizz until well blended and fairly smooth.

3 Spoon into a small bowl and serve with sticks of raw vegetables and whatever else you like.

Croque Monsieur

The French know how to spoil themselves and this wonderfully wicked, indulgent snack, brunch or lunch is great for hungry teenagers. Choose good-quality ham, ideally hand-carved from a freshly cooked joint. And if you sit a fried egg on top of the sandwich it becomes a croque Madame!

SERVES 2

50g (2oz) butter
4 medium slices of white bread
2 tbsp Dijon mustard
4 thin slices of smoked ham
100g (4oz) Gruyère cheese, coarsely grated
15g (½oz) plain flour
150ml (5fl oz) hot full-fat milk
Freshly grated nutmeg
Salt and freshly ground black pepper

PREPARE AHEAD
Can be assembled up to an hour ahead, ready to grill.

1   You will need a baking sheet lined with foil. Preheat the grill to a medium setting.

2   Melt half the butter in a small saucepan, then brush it over one side of each slice of bread. Place the bread on the baking sheet, buttered side up. Grill for 1–2 minutes until lightly golden.

3   Turn the bread over and spread the unbuttered side with Dijon mustard. Put two slices of ham on the mustard side of two of the slices of bread. Top this with 50g (2oz) of the grated cheese and then cover with the remaining slices of bread, toasted side up, to make two sandwiches.

4   Melt the remaining butter in the saucepan and whisk in the flour with a small sauce whisk. Heat for a few seconds, then whisk in the hot milk. Once the sauce has thickened, remove the pan from the heat and add a little nutmeg and 25g (1oz) of the cheese. Season well – this will be a very thick cheese sauce.

5   Spread the sauce over the top of both sandwiches and sprinkle with the remaining 25g (1oz) of cheese. Put back under the hot grill for about 5 minutes until the cheese has melted in the middle and the top is golden brown and bubbling. Leave for a few seconds before slicing in half, then serve immediately.

Burrata with heritage tomato salad & Bloody Mary dressing

I find this is one of the most popular sharing plates – just break the burrata open and let everyone help themselves. Burrata, which means 'buttery' in Italian, is a fresh cheese made from a mix of mozzarella and cream. It's shaped like a ball and the outside thin shell is buffalo or cow's milk mozzarella, while the inside contains a soft, doughy, stringy mixture of curd and fresh cream. It's best served at room temperature.

SERVES 6

750g (1¾lb) heritage tomatoes,
    mixed sizes and colours
1 x 320g (11oz) burrata ball
1 small bunch of basil, leaves
    torn into pieces
1 celery stick, with leaves
Coarse sea salt and freshly
    ground black pepper

FOR THE DRESSING
75ml (3fl oz) tomato juice
4 tbsp olive oil
1 tsp Worcestershire sauce
2 tsp balsamic vinegar
Tabasco sauce, to taste
Celery salt, to taste

PREPARE AHEAD
*Assemble the salad up to 2 hours
ahead and dress just before serving.
The dressing can be made up to
a day ahead.*

1 Roughly slice the tomatoes into different shapes and sizes.

2 Place the burrata in the centre of a serving dish. Arrange the various tomatoes around the cheese and sprinkle with basil leaves.

3 For the dressing, mix the tomato juice, oil, Worcestershire sauce and vinegar in a jug and season well with Tabasco, celery salt and pepper.

4 To serve, season the tomatoes with coarse sea salt and pepper and pour over a little of the dressing. Serve the rest of the dressing in a jug. Add the celery stick and use it to stir the dressing just before serving with some crusty bread.

Toasted muffins with scrambled eggs & smoked salmon

Brunch is becoming more and more popular and this is a perfect quick dish.
You can swap the smoked salmon for crispy bacon if you prefer.

SERVES 4

2 English muffins

4 eggs

A knob of butter, plus extra
  for spreading

1 tbsp pouring double cream

2 tsp snipped chives

4 small slices of smoked salmon

A squeeze of lemon juice

Salt and freshly ground black
  pepper

1 Slice the muffins in half and toast them until golden.

2 Break the eggs into a bowl, season with salt and black pepper,
   then beat with a fork.

3 Heat the knob of butter in a non-stick pan, add the scrambled
   egg mixture and cook over a low heat. Stir in the cream and chives
   and cook for couple of minutes until soft and creamy. Be careful
   not to overcook and remember that the eggs will continue to cook
   in the hot pan, even when it is taken off the heat.

4 Spread the toasted muffins with a little butter and divide the
   scrambled eggs between them. Sit a twist of salmon on each one,
   then add a squeeze of lemon and some pepper. Serve immediately.

Poultry & Game

Preserved lemon chicken

This simple casserole is full of flavour. You can use chicken thighs if you prefer,
but you will need to cook them for 10 minutes longer.

SERVES 4

4 small skinless and boneless
   chicken breasts
2 tbsp olive oil
2 onions, roughly chopped
1 garlic clove, crushed
1cm (½in) knob of fresh root
   ginger, finely grated
1 tsp ground cumin
200ml (7fl oz) white wine
350ml (12fl oz) chicken stock
2 tbsp tomato purée
1 tbsp runny honey
2 preserved lemons, chopped
1 tbsp cornflour
2 tbsp chopped parsley or
   coriander
Salt and freshly ground black
   pepper

PREPARE AHEAD
*Can be made up to 2 days
ahead and reheated.*

FREEZE
Freezes well.

1 You will need a deep frying pan or sauté pan with a lid or a
flameproof casserole dish.

2 Season the chicken breasts. Heat the oil in the pan and fry the
chicken breasts over a high heat until golden brown all over, then
set them aside.

3 Add the onions to the pan and fry for a minute. Lower the heat,
cover the pan with a lid and cook for about 5 minutes. Add the
garlic and ginger, sprinkle in the cumin and fry for 30 seconds.
Stir in the wine and boil for 2 minutes. Add the stock and purée
and bring back to the boil. Stir in the honey and preserved lemons
and season with salt and pepper.

4 Return the chicken to the pan, cover and bring back to the boil.
Lower the heat and leave to simmer gently on the hob for about
20–25 minutes until the chicken is cooked through.

5 Mix the cornflour with 3 tablespoons of cold water in a small
bowl. Add a little of the hot chicken stock and mix well. Add the
cornflour mixture to the pan, bring to the boil and stir over the
heat until the sauce has thickened. Check the seasoning.

6 Sprinkle with parsley or coriander, then serve with mashed potato
or rice, and fresh greens.

Roast chicken with tarragon butter & melting onions

Roast chicken seems to me to be the ultimate comfort meal for all the family. It's something everyone loves and it brings family and friends together to share stories and memories.

SERVES 6

50g (2oz) butter, softened
1 garlic clove, crushed
2cm (¾in) knob of fresh root ginger, finely grated
1 tbsp chopped tarragon
Zest of ½ lemon
1.8–2kg (4–4½lb) free-range oven-ready chicken
2 large onions, very thickly sliced
Olive oil, for drizzling
Salt and freshly ground black pepper

FOR THE GRAVY

50g (2oz) flour
100ml (3½fl oz) white wine
500ml (17fl oz) chicken stock
Worcestershire sauce, to taste
1 tbsp redcurrant jelly
Gravy browning (optional)
1 tbsp chopped tarragon

1 Preheat the oven to 200°C/180°C fan/Gas 6.

2 Measure the butter, garlic, ginger, tarragon and lemon zest into a small bowl, season and mix well. Place the chicken on a board. Loosen the skin over the breast and pull it up to make a pocket (but do not pull the skin off). Push the butter mixture under the skin and use your hand to spread the mixture out into an even layer. Push the skin back down. Put any tarragon stalks into the cavity of the chicken.

3 Transfer the chicken to a roasting tin and scatter the onions around it. Drizzle a little oil over the skin and legs, rub it in, then season the chicken with salt and pepper. Roast in the oven for about 1½ hours.

4 To test if the chicken is cooked, insert a small, sharp knife or a skewer into the thickest part of the thigh; if the juices run clear, it is done. Transfer the chicken to a board, cover with foil and leave to rest for 5 minutes. Spoon the onions into a hot serving bowl.

5 Place the roasting tin with the cooking juices over a medium heat. Sprinkle over the flour and whisk until smooth. Add the wine, stock, Worcestershire sauce, redcurrant jelly and the gravy browning, if using. Whisk over the heat for 5 minutes until well combined and thickened. Check the seasoning, pour the gravy through a sieve into a warm jug and stir in the tarragon.

6 Carve the chicken and serve with the meltingly soft onions.

Chicken hot pot with potato topping

Hearty, healthy and wholesome, this is perfect bowl food, so ideal for an informal gathering. Once the dish is cooked, there is lots of tasty sauce – delicious for mopping up with a piece of crusty bread.

SERVES 6

50g (2oz) butter

2 onions, thinly sliced

2 celery sticks, thinly sliced

2 carrots, peeled and cut into small cubes

50g (2oz) plain flour

100ml (3½fl oz) white wine

450ml (15fl oz) hot chicken stock

1 tbsp tomato purée

750g (1¾lb) skinless and boneless chicken thighs, sliced into 4cm (1½in) pieces

200g (7oz) small chestnut mushrooms, thickly sliced

1 tbsp chopped thyme

2 bay leaves

750g (1¾lb) large potatoes, peeled and sliced into very thin discs

Salt and freshly ground black pepper

PREPARE AHEAD
Can be made up to 6 hours ahead. Reheat gently on the hob until hot, then finish off under the grill.

1 Preheat the oven to 180°C/160°C fan/Gas 4. You will need a large flameproof and ovenproof casserole dish with a lid.

2 Melt the butter in the casserole dish. Add the onions, celery and carrots and cook over a high heat for a few minutes, turning them frequently.

3 Measure the flour into a bowl, gradually pour in the wine and whisk until smooth. Pour in a little of the hot stock and mix again, then add the remaining stock and whisk until smooth. Add the liquid to the vegetables in the dish and stir in the tomato purée. Bring to the boil, then add the chicken, mushrooms, thyme and bay leaves. Season with salt and pepper.

4 Arrange the potatoes in a neat layer over the top, slightly overlapping the slices. Season with salt and pepper and gently push the slices down into the sauce a little.

5 Cover the dish with a lid and bake in the oven for about an hour, until everything is tender and cooked through.

6 Preheat the grill, take the dish out of the oven and remove the lid. Place the dish under the grill for 5-10 minutes until the potatoes are golden. Serve hot, with some green vegetables.

Mild curried chicken with grapes & asparagus

Grapes are an ingredient we used to add to chicken dishes in the 1980s. I'd forgotten how good the combination was until I was at a friend's house recently and was served such a dish. Here is an updated version of a classic chicken Véronique.

SERVES 6

750g (1¾lb) chicken thighs, skin on and bone in (about 8 large thighs)
1 carrot, peeled and sliced
1 onion, sliced
3 cloves
2 bay leaves
1 tsp salt
6 black peppercorns
1 chicken stock cube
200g (7oz) asparagus spears
100g (4oz) seedless green grapes, halved
Salt and freshly ground black pepper

FOR THE SAUCE
25g (1oz) butter
2 tsp curry powder
25g (1oz) flour
2 tsp redcurrant jelly
200g (7oz) full-fat crème fraîche

PREPARE AHEAD
Can be made up to a day ahead, but add the asparagus and grapes on the day.

FREEZE
The chicken in the sauce freezes well.

1 To poach the chicken, place the thighs in a small pan. Add the carrot, onion, cloves, bay leaves, salt and peppercorns. Pour cold water over the chicken thighs so they are just covered and add the chicken stock cube.

2 Cover the pan with a lid, bring to the boil and boil for about 5 minutes. Lower the heat and leave to simmer gently for about 45 minutes until the chicken is tender. Remove the chicken thighs from the pan and sit them on a board. Strain the stock through a colander and reserve it for the sauce. Remove the skin and bone from the chicken thighs and slice each thigh in half. Keep the chicken warm while you cook the asparagus and make the sauce.

3 Snap off the woody ends of the asparagus spears. Cook the asparagus for 3 minutes in boiling water, then drain. Slice the spears into rounds, leaving the tips 5cm (2in) long.

4 For the sauce, melt the butter in a saucepan, sprinkle in the curry powder and stir for a few seconds over a high heat. Add the flour and stir for a more few seconds. Gradually pour in 300ml (10fl oz) of the reserved stock and whisk until smooth and thickened. You may have some poaching liquid left over, but this can be frozen for another time.

5 Whisk the redcurrant jelly and crème fraîche into the sauce until smooth. Add the chicken, stir and bring back to the boil. Season and tip into a warm, wide-based heatproof dish. Spread the chicken out in the dish, then scatter the grapes and asparagus over the top. Serve hot, with rice.

Five-spiced chicken with coriander & cucumber relish

Teenagers will love this recipe, which is great for serving a crowd. There's a nice bit of spice and it can be served with wraps, jacket potatoes, rice or a grain salad, with a tomato salad alongside. Peppadew peppers come in a jar, mild or hot; mild is best for this dish.

SERVES 4

1 tsp Chinese five spice powder
4 peppadew peppers, chopped
3cm (1½in) knob of fresh root
   ginger, grated
3 tbsp sunflower oil
Juice of ½ lemon
4 small skinless and boneless
   chicken breasts, sliced
   in half widthways
Salt and freshly ground black
   pepper

FOR THE CORIANDER
& CUCUMBER RELISH
Bunch of coriander, roughly
   chopped
½ cucumber, peeled, deseeded
   and finely diced
2 tbsp mango chutney
Juice of 1 small lemon
2 peppadew peppers, chopped

PREPARE AHEAD
Marinate the chicken up to 12 hours ahead. Relish can be made up to a day ahead.

1 To make the marinade for the chicken, measure the five spice powder, peppers, ginger, 2 tablespoons of the oil and the lemon juice into a bowl and mix to combine.

2 Put the chicken pieces on a board. Cover them with baking paper and bash with a rolling pin until they are about 1–2cm (½–¾in) thick. Put into the marinade, stir to coat and leave for an hour (or up to 12 hours).

3 To make the relish, measure all the ingredients into a bowl and mix to combine. Season with salt and pepper to taste.

4 Heat a large frying pan and add the remaining tablespoon of oil. Season the chicken, then fry for 4–5 minutes each side until cooked through and golden brown. Arrange the chicken on a warm serving dish with the relish alongside and a tomato salad.

Mexican chicken & avocado sharing platter

It's great to make your own wraps for this sharing dish, but you can buy tortilla wraps if you prefer. There are more wrap recipes on pages 62 and 171.

SERVES 6

FOR THE WRAPS
250g (9oz) plain flour
25g (1oz) butter, cubed
½ tsp salt
1 tsp bicarbonate of soda
150ml (5fl oz) warm water

FOR THE SPICED CHICKEN
Zest and juice of 1 lime
1 garlic clove, crushed
2 tsp paprika
2 tsp ground cumin
2 tbsp sunflower oil
2 large skinless and boneless
   chicken breasts
2 red peppers, deseeded and sliced
1 large red onion, thinly sliced
Salt and black pepper

FOR THE AVOCADO SALSA
250g (9oz) cherry tomatoes
1 avocado, peeled and diced
½ fresh green chilli, deseeded
   and finely diced
Juice of ½ lemon

TO SERVE
100g (4oz) mature Cheddar
   cheese, grated
3 tbsp soured cream

PREPARE AHEAD
Marinate the chicken up to 12 hours
ahead. Wraps can be made up to 6
hours ahead and warmed to serve.
Avocado salsa keeps for 8 hours.

1 Measure the flour, butter, salt and bicarbonate of soda into a large mixing bowl. Rub in the butter with your fingertips until the mixture looks like crumbs. Add the water and mix with a knife to bring the dough together.

2 Knead lightly into a soft dough, then divide into 6 balls. Dust the work surface with flour and roll out each ball of dough into a large thin round about the size of a dinner plate. Heat a frying pan until very hot. Fry the wraps one at a time until slightly golden, but not crisp, and set aside.

3 For the chicken marinade, measure the lime zest and juice, garlic, spices and oil into a bowl and whisk until combined. Add the chicken, toss to coat in the marinade, then cover the bowl and leave to marinate for 10 minutes or up to 8 hours.

4 Slice the chicken into thin strips. Heat a large frying pan. Add the chicken and fry briefly over a high heat until golden brown and just cooked, then transfer to a plate. Wipe out the pan – this is important, otherwise the residue will burn. Add a little oil to the pan and fry the peppers and onion for 5–6 minutes until just tender. Return the chicken to the pan and toss over the heat for a few minutes. Season and spoon into a warm serving bowl.

5 For the salsa, slice each tomato into 8 and put them in a bowl with the avocado, chilli and lemon juice. Season with salt and pepper and stir to combine, then spoon into a small serving bowl.

6 Warm the wraps in a non-stick pan for a few moments and put the cheese and soured cream into small dishes. Serve with the chicken, so everyone can help themselves.

Sri Lankan chicken curry

My husband spent many years in Sri Lanka and this is his favourite comforting curry, which brings back very happy memories. The curry paste is quick to make and well worth it for the flavour.

SERVES 4

FOR THE FRESH CURRY PASTE
4 large black cardamom pods
2 tsp fennel seeds
2 tsp ground cumin
2 tsp ground coriander
1 tsp turmeric
1 fresh green chilli, deseeded
    and chopped
2 garlic cloves, sliced
2cm (¾in) knob of fresh root
    ginger, peeled and chopped
2 tbsp sunflower oil

FOR THE CHICKEN
2 tbsp sunflower oil
4 skinless and boneless chicken
    breasts, diced
2 large onions, sliced
1 red pepper, deseeded and diced
400g (14oz) tin of chopped
    tomatoes
5 dried curry leaves (optional)
1 tbsp light muscovado sugar
400g (14oz) tin of full-fat
    coconut milk
Juice of ½ lime
Bunch of coriander, chopped
Salt and freshly ground black
    pepper

PREPARE AHEAD
*Can be made up to a day
ahead and reheated to serve.*

1 You will need a deep frying pan or sauté pan with a lid or a flameproof and ovenproof casserole dish.

2 For the curry paste, use a rolling pin to bash the cardamom pods and release the seeds, then place the seeds in a mortar. Add the fennel seeds and grind with a pestle to a fine powder. If you do not have a pestle and mortar, crush the seeds in a small bag with a rolling pin. Put the cardamon and fennel seeds in a small blender with all the other curry paste ingredients and whizz to make a smooth paste.

3 Heat your pan until hot and add the oil. Season the chicken and fry it quickly over a high heat until browned. Remove the chicken with a slotted spoon and set aside.

4 Add the onions and pepper to the unwashed pan and fry for 5 minutes. Stir in the curry paste and fry for 30 seconds, then add the tomatoes, curry leaves, if using, the sugar and 150ml (5fl oz) of water. Stir, cover the pan with a lid and simmer for 15–20 minutes until the vegetables are soft.

5 Pour in the coconut milk, bring to the boil and cook for about 5 minutes until the sauce has reduced and thickened. Return the chicken to the pan, cover with a lid and gently simmer for about 5–8 minutes until the chicken is cooked through.

6 Add the lime juice, season with salt and pepper and remove the curry leaves, if used. Stir in the chopped coriander just before serving the curry hot, with rice.

Warm chicken Caesar, bacon & avocado wraps

These go well with the bean and butternut squash wraps on page 171 and with the Mexican wraps on page 59. They're good to serve together for a family lunch.

MAKES 4

2 rashers of smoked back bacon, cut widthways into pieces
1 large cooked chicken breast, sliced into thin strips
4 wraps
1 small romaine lettuce, finely sliced
1 small ripe avocado, peeled and sliced
3 tbsp mayonnaise
1 tbsp lemon juice
25g (1oz) Parmesan cheese, grated
2 tsp snipped chives
Salt and freshly ground black pepper

1 Heat a frying pan and add the bacon. Allow the fat to run out and fry the bacon until crisp, then add the strips of chicken and stir to heat them through. Transfer to a plate.

2 Warm the wraps in the empty frying pan on the hob.

3 Put some lettuce in the centre of each wrap and top with chicken, bacon and avocado.

4 Measure the mayonnaise into a small bowl and add the lemon juice, Parmesan and chives. Season with a little salt and pepper and stir to combine, then spoon some of the lemon and Parmesan mayonnaise mixture on top of the chicken.

5 Fold up the bottom of each wrap, then turn in the sides. Roll up tightly and slice in half on the diagonal.

Open chicken, bacon & avocado sandwich with maple dressing

A sandwich makes such a comforting lunch and this is an excellent one to choose. I do like open sandwiches, as they give double the amount of tasty topping and use less bread.

MAKES 2 OPEN SANDWICHES

1 small chicken breast
2 rashers of smoked streaky
   bacon
2 slices of granary bread
1 tbsp mayonnaise
½ ripe avocado, peeled and sliced
Salt and freshly ground black
   pepper
Coriander leaves, to garnish

FOR THE MAPLE DRESSING
Zest and juice of ½ lime
1 tsp maple syrup
2 tbsp olive oil

PREPARE AHEAD
*Dressing can be made
3 days ahead.*

1   Measure the dressing ingredients into a small jug, whisk until combined and season with salt and pepper. Put a tablespoon of the dressing into a bowl.

2   Place the chicken on a board and cover it with cling film. Using a rolling pin, bash the chicken breast until it is about a third of its original thickness, then slice in half lengthways and season. Add the chicken to the bowl of dressing and leave to marinate for about 10 minutes.

3   Heat a frying pan over a high heat, add the bacon and fry until crisp on both sides, then set aside. Add the chicken to the pan and fry for about 2 minutes on both sides until golden and cooked through. Slice the chicken into strips, then set it aside with the bacon to keep warm.

4   Toast the slices of bread and spread them with mayonnaise. Arrange the avocado slices on top, then add the chicken and bacon. Garnish with coriander and drizzle with the remaining dressing. Serve at once.

Smoky firecracker chicken drumsticks

Simple food that can be hand-held like these drumsticks is perfect for a November evening, sitting round a bonfire with the children. The sweet smoked paprika gives a lovely woody taste.

SERVES 4–6

12 chicken drumsticks

FOR THE MARINADE

2 tbsp sweet smoked paprika

2 tbsp Worcestershire sauce

2 tbsp maple syrup

6 tbsp olive oil

2 garlic cloves, crushed

Tabasco sauce, to taste

Salt and freshly ground black pepper

PREPARE AHEAD

Can be marinated up to a day ahead.

FREEZE

Freezes well once marinated.

1 Preheat the oven to 220°C/200°C fan/Gas 7. Line a large roasting tin with non-stick baking paper.

2 Measure the marinade ingredients into a bowl and mix well, then season with salt and pepper. Add the chicken drumsticks and leave to marinate for 30 minutes, or longer if you have time.

3 Lay the drumsticks in the roasting tin, then pour over the marinade, brushing it around both sides of the chicken. Roast in the oven for 30–40 minutes until golden and cooked through.

Stir-fried chicken & vegetable rice

This is an everyday dish that is simple and warming, so just right when the nights draw in and you want an easy but tasty family supper. Cooking the rice in stock rather than water gives a great depth of flavour.

SERVES 4–6

225g (8oz) long-grain rice
500ml (16fl oz) chicken stock
3 tbsp sunflower oil
2 skinless and boneless chicken
   breasts, sliced into small strips
1 tbsp runny honey
3 rashers of unsmoked bacon,
   cut into pieces
1 large onion, finely chopped
1 red pepper, deseeded and
   thinly sliced
200g (7oz) button mushrooms,
   sliced
2 garlic cloves, crushed
100g (4oz) frozen petits pois
2 tbsp Worcestershire sauce
A large knob of butter
Salt and freshly ground black
   pepper

1 Measure the rice and stock into a wide-based saucepan. Cover with a lid and bring to the boil. Simmer for about 15 minutes over a low heat until all the stock has been absorbed, or cook according to the packet instructions. Set the rice aside.

2 Heat a tablespoon of the oil in a large frying pan. Toss the chicken strips in the honey and fry over a high heat until golden all over. Remove with a slotted spoon and set aside. Add the bacon pieces and fry until crisp, then remove and set aside with the chicken.

3 Add the remaining oil to the pan. Add the onion and pepper and fry for about 3 minutes. Add the mushrooms and garlic and fry until the mushrooms are lightly browned. Tip in the cooked rice, add the peas and Worcestershire sauce, then toss over the heat.

4 Return the chicken and bacon to the pan, stir in the butter to enrich and season with salt and pepper. Serve as it is, or with a dressed leaf salad.

Chicken & fennel fricassee with tarragon

We often have friends round for a midweek supper and this is a perfect dish to make ahead! We like chicken thighs, skinned but left on the bone for full flavour, but you could also use skinned chicken breasts. These only need to cook for 30 minutes.

SERVES 4–6

2 tbsp olive oil
8 bone-in chicken thighs or
 6 chicken breasts, skinned
2 onions, cut into thin wedges
2 fennel bulbs, trimmed and
 thickly sliced
100ml (3½ fl oz) dry sherry
200ml (7fl oz) chicken stock
2 tbsp cornflour
200g (7oz) full-fat crème fraîche
Small bunch of tarragon,
 chopped
½ tsp caster sugar
Juice of ½ lemon
Salt and freshly ground black
 pepper

PREPARE AHEAD
*Can be made up to a day ahead,
but add the tarragon once reheated.*

FREEZE
Freezes well.

1 You will need a deep sauté pan or frying pan with a lid or a flameproof and ovenproof casserole dish. Preheat the oven to 160°C/140°C fan/Gas 3.

2 Heat the pan until hot, then add the oil. Season the chicken and fry quickly over a high heat until golden and sealed all over. Remove and set aside.

3 Add the onions and fennel to the unwashed pan and fry for about 5 minutes, stirring. Pour in the sherry and boil over a high heat to reduce by half. Pour in the stock, return the chicken to the pan, then season with salt and pepper. Bring to the boil, cover with a lid and transfer to the oven. Cook for about 45 minutes or until the chicken is tender (about 30 minutes if using breasts).

4 Measure the cornflour into a small bowl, add a little cold water and stir until smooth.

5 Transfer the pan to the hob, remove the lid and stir in the crème fraîche. Then add the cornflour mixture and stir over the heat until the sauce has thickened. Add the tarragon, sugar and lemon juice and check for seasoning. Serve piping hot, with rice or mash and heaps of wilted spinach.

Warm chicken & dill salad with mustard Parmesan dressing

If you are a fan of Caesar salad this is a great recipe to try – but you must like dill to enjoy it! Crunchy lettuce is best here, as it keeps firm and crisp.

SERVES 4–6

2 skinless and boneless chicken
   breasts, cut into thin strips
1 tbsp paprika
1 tsp runny honey
2 tbsp olive oil
Salt and freshly ground black
   pepper

FOR THE SALAD
½ large iceberg lettuce, very
   finely shredded
1 large bunch of dill, leaves
   removed and chopped
6 spring onions, thinly sliced
6 dill pickles or gherkins (from
   a jar), finely chopped

FOR THE DRESSING
200g (7oz) full-fat crème fraîche
Juice of 1 large lemon
2 tsp Dijon mustard
1 tsp sugar
25g (1oz) Parmesan cheese,
   finely grated

TO SERVE
1 heaped tbsp Parmesan shavings
25g (1oz) pea shoots or
   microherbs, to decorate

PREPARE AHEAD
Dressing can be made up to a day
ahead. Assemble the salad up to 2 hours
ahead and dress just before serving.

1 Put the chicken into a bowl with the paprika, honey and a tablespoon of the oil. Season well and toss to coat all the chicken pieces.

2 Heat a large frying pan and add the remaining oil. Fry the chicken pieces briefly over a high heat until golden brown and just cooked through – take care not to overcook them. Remove to a plate, cover with foil and leave to rest for 5 minutes.

3 Scatter the lettuce over a large serving plate and sprinkle with the dill, spring onions and pickles. Arrange the warm chicken pieces on top.

4 Measure all the dressing ingredients into a bowl and whisk until combined. Check the seasoning. Pour the dressing over the salad and sprinkle with Parmesan shavings and microherbs.

Duck salad with hoisin dressing

Using the classic Chinese flavours of cucumber, spring onion, duck and hoisin sauce, and with the addition of fresh watermelon, this is a very different salad.

SERVES 4

1 tsp sunflower oil
2 small duck breasts, skinned
Salt and freshly ground black
   pepper

FOR THE SALAD
½ small cucumber
2 large Little Gem lettuces,
   broken into pieces
4 spring onions, sliced
Small bunch of coriander,
   chopped
2 tbsp chopped mint
500g (1lb 2oz) watermelon,
   deseeded and cubed

FOR THE DRESSING
3 tbsp hoisin sauce
Juice of 2 limes
4 tbsp sunflower oil
Light muscovado sugar, to taste
1 tbsp soy sauce
½ garlic clove, crushed

PREPARE AHEAD
Dressing can be made up to
2 days ahead. Assemble the dish
up to 4 hours ahead, then dress
just before serving.

1 Heat a small frying pan and add the oil. Season the duck breasts and fry them over a high heat until both sides are golden. Lower the heat and continue to cook the breasts for about 3 minutes on each side until just cooked but still pink in the middle.

2 For the salad, cut the cucumber in half lengthways. Take a teaspoon, drag it along the centre to remove all the seeds and discard them. Sit the cucumber cut side down on a board and slice into fairly thin horseshoe shapes. Tip these into a bowl and mix with the rest of the salad ingredients. Arrange the salad on a serving platter.

3 Thinly slice the duck and arrange it on top of the salad.

4 Measure the dressing ingredients into a small jar, screw on the lid and shake until well mixed. Pour half the dressing over the salad when you are ready to eat and serve the rest in a jug.

Pheasant & port stew

Hearty and welcoming, this stew is perfect in autumn when pheasants are in season and leeks are at their best. Be careful not to overcook the pheasant breasts, as they will become too dry.

SERVES 6

1 tbsp sunflower oil
A large knob of butter
6 pheasant breasts, skinned
3 leeks, thinly sliced
3 celery sticks, thinly sliced
2 garlic cloves, crushed
50g (2oz) plain flour
200ml (7fl oz) port
450ml (15fl oz) chicken or game
  stock
3 bay leaves
1 tbsp balsamic vinegar
2 tbsp soy sauce
1 tbsp sun-dried tomato paste
Salt and freshly ground black
  pepper

PREPARE AHEAD
Can be made up to a day ahead and reheated to serve.

FREEZE
Freezes well.

1 You will need a large deep sauté pan or frying pan with a lid, or a flameproof and ovenproof casserole dish. Preheat the oven to 160°C/140°C fan/Gas 3.

2 Heat the pan and add the oil and butter. Season the pheasant breasts and brown over a high heat until golden on all sides. Remove and set aside.

3 Add the leeks and celery to the pan and fry over a medium heat for about 4–5 minutes. Add the garlic and cook for 30 seconds, stirring. Measure the flour into a medium bowl, add the port and whisk until smooth. Whisk in the stock.

4 Add the stock and port mixture to the pan, bring to the boil and keep stirring until thickened. Add the bay leaves, season with salt and pepper and return the pheasant to the pan. Cover the pan with a lid, transfer to the oven and cook for about 20–30 minutes until the breasts are tender. Stir in the vinegar, soy sauce and tomato paste, then bring to the boil and cook for 3–4 minutes.

5 Serve with potato or celeriac mash and green vegetables.

Spiced quail with coriander dressing

This recipe has a hint of the Middle East and is perfect served with bowl of couscous or other grains. It also works well with large chicken thighs, bone in but skinned.

SERVES 4

4 oven-ready quail
2 large onions, thinly sliced
3 celery sticks, thickly sliced
3 tbsp olive oil
3 tbsp chopped coriander
Salt and freshly ground black
    pepper

FOR THE SPICED MARINADE
2 tbsp mango chutney
1 small garlic clove, crushed
1 tsp sweet smoked paprika
½ tsp ground cumin
½ tsp ground coriander
½ tsp ground ginger
½ tsp cinnamon
Juice of ½ lemon

FOR THE CORIANDER
DRESSING
150g (5oz) natural yoghurt
2 tbsp finely chopped coriander
1 tbsp mint sauce
¼ cucumber, coarsely grated
1 tbsp chopped fresh mint

PREPARE AHEAD
Quail can be marinated up to a day before. Dressing can be made up to 2 days ahead.

FREEZE
Raw quail freeze well in the marinade.

1 Measure all the marinade ingredients into a large bowl. Mix well, then add the quail, onions and celery and stir to coat them in the marinade. Leave to marinate overnight or for as long as time allows.

2 Preheat the oven to 200°C/180°C fan/Gas 6. Heat a tablespoon of the oil in a frying pan. Remove the quail from the marinade, add them to the pan and brown well over a high heat until golden all over. Sit the quail, breast side up, in a large roasting tin and spoon the vegetables and marinade around them.

3 Season with salt and pepper and drizzle the rest of the oil over the breasts of the birds. Roast the quail for about 25–30 minutes or until cooked through. Arrange the quail on a platter, spoon the vegetables around them and sprinkle over the fresh coriander.

4 Mix the ingredients for the dressing in a jug and season with salt and pepper. Spoon the dressing over the quail or serve alongside.

Fish & Seafood

Crab linguine

Use fresh, frozen or canned white crabmeat for this recipe. The dark crabmeat
is not suitable, as it is too strong and discolours the pasta.

SERVES 4

350g (12oz) linguine

4 tbsp olive oil, plus extra for
drizzling

6 spring onions, thinly sliced

1 large fresh red chilli, deseeded
and diced

1 garlic clove, crushed

3cm (1¼in) knob of fresh root
ginger, finely grated

300g (11oz) white crabmeat

Juice of 2 limes

Large bunch of coriander,
chopped

Salt and freshly ground black
pepper

1 Cook the pasta in boiling salted water according to the packet
instructions, then drain, reserving 100ml (3½fl oz) of the pasta
cooking water.

2 Heat the oil in a large frying pan. Add the spring onions, chilli,
garlic and ginger, then fry for 2 minutes. Stir in the crab and heat
for 2 minutes – try not to break up the crab too much.

3 Add the pasta, reserved pasta water, lime juice and coriander.
Season well and gently toss everything together over a medium
heat. Serve at once, drizzled with a little olive oil.

Crab & herb blinis with pickled fennel salad

Delicious for lunch or a light supper, this combines beautifully light blinis with fresh crab and a sharp fennel salad that cuts through the richness of the shellfish. If fresh crabmeat is not available, use thawed frozen crabmeat.

SERVES 4

FOR THE FENNEL SALAD
15g (½oz) light muscovado sugar
25ml (1fl oz) white wine vinegar
1 fennel bulb, core removed
1 spring onion, finely sliced
½ tsp chopped tarragon leaves
1 tbsp chopped dill
Salt and black pepper

FOR THE HERB BLINIS
100g (4oz) self-raising flour
½ tsp baking powder
1 egg, beaten
About 125ml (4fl oz) milk
1 tbsp chopped dill
2 tsp snipped chives
Vegetable oil, for frying

FOR THE CRAB TOPPING
2 tbsp full-fat crème fraîche
2 tsp fresh lemon juice
2 spring onions, chopped
2 tsp hot horseradish sauce
2 tbsp chopped dill
1 tbsp chopped parsley
Tabasco sauce, to taste
200g (7oz) fresh white crabmeat
Pea shoots, to garnish

PREPARE AHEAD
Can make all the components up to 8 hours ahead, then assemble up to an hour before serving.

1   For the salad, measure the sugar and wine vinegar into a small pan. Heat gently, stirring, until the sugar has dissolved, then pour into a salad bowl and leave to cool. Slice the fennel as thinly as you can and add it to the bowl with the spring onions, herbs and seasoning. Stir to combine and leave to marinate for about an hour.

2   For the blinis, measure the flour and baking powder into a mixing bowl. Add the egg and a little of the milk, then whisk to combine. Gradually whisk in the remaining milk to make a smooth batter with the consistency of thick pouring cream. Add the herbs and season with salt and pepper.

3   Heat a frying pan until hot and add little oil. Spoon in a heaped tablespoon of batter to make a large thin blini – almost like a Scotch pancake. Cook for a few minutes and when bubbles start to appear on the surface, flip it over and cook for 1–2 minutes until cooked through. Repeat with the remaining mixture to make 4 blinis. Set them aside on a rack to cool.

4   To make the crab topping, mix the crème fraîche, lemon juice, spring onions, horseradish, herbs and Tabasco in a bowl, then season with salt and pepper. Reserve a heaped tablespoon of crabmeat and mix the rest into the bowl.

5   Sit each blini on a plate. Divide the crab mixture between them and spoon a little of the reserved crab in the centre of each. Spoon the salad next to the blinis and garnish with pea shoots.

Hot smoked salmon & asparagus salad

Hot smoked salmon comes in packs and has the texture of flaked poached salmon and the taste of smoked salmon. It makes a wonderful, colourful salad that's full of flavour.

SERVES 4–6

400g (14oz) asparagus spears, trimmed
4 large eggs
1 ripe avocado, peeled and thinly sliced
Juice of ½ lemon
150g (5oz) hot smoked salmon
2 Little Gem lettuces, broken into pieces
Handful of lamb's lettuce
Salt and freshly ground black pepper

FOR THE FENNEL MUSTARD DRESSING
1 tbsp Dijon mustard
1 tbsp grainy mustard
2 tbsp white wine vinegar
8 tbsp olive oil
2 tbsp runny honey
2 tbsp mayonnaise
1 small fennel bulb, core removed, very thinly sliced

PREPARE AHEAD
Dressing can be made up to 8 hours ahead. Assemble the salad up to 6 hours ahead and dress just before serving.

1 Cook the asparagus in a pan of boiling salted water for 3–4 minutes, according to the size of the spears. Drain them and run under cold water to set the colour and stop the cooking, then dry well on kitchen paper. Slice the stems into rounds and keep the tips whole.

2 Put the eggs into a saucepan of cold water, bring to the boil and boil for 8 minutes. Drain and run the eggs under cold water. Peel the eggs and slice each one into quarters. Toss the slices of avocado in lemon juice.

3 Gently break the salmon into small pieces. Break the leaves from the lettuces into bite-sized pieces. Scatter the lettuce and lamb's lettuce into a large wide bowl. Arrange the asparagus over them, place the egg quarters evenly on top and scatter over the salmon, seasoning each layer with salt and pepper.

4 Measure all the dressing ingredients into a bowl. Whisk until combined and season with salt and pepper. Add the fennel and stir to coat.

5 When ready to serve, pour half the dressing over the salad and toss very gently. Serve the rest of the dressing in a small jug.

Grilled garlic prawns
& Mediterranean vegetables

This is such a luxury and so indulgent. In this dish, keeping things simple
is the key to enjoying the best-flavoured ingredients.

SERVES 4

12 raw tiger prawns, shells
  and heads on, or the largest
  prawns you can buy
Juice of ½ lemon
1 tbsp thyme leaves
Salt and freshly ground black
  pepper
Lemon wedges, to serve

FOR THE GARLIC BUTTER
25g (1oz) butter, softened
1 garlic clove, crushed

FOR THE VEGETABLES
2 tbsp olive oil, plus extra
  for greasing
1 garlic clove, crushed
1 tbsp balsamic glaze
1 tsp runny honey
1 fennel bulb, halved, cored
  and thinly sliced
200g (7oz) baby courgettes,
  sliced into rounds
2 red or yellow Romano
  peppers, deseeded and sliced
  into large pieces

1 Preheat the grill to high. Mix the butter and garlic in a small
   bowl and mash with a fork until combined.

2 For the vegetables, mix the olive oil, garlic, balsamic and honey
   together in a large bowl and add the fennel, courgettes and
   peppers. Toss to coat all the vegetables and leave to marinate
   for 10 minutes. Season well.

3 Grease a baking sheet with oil. Arrange the vegetables on the
   baking sheet and pour over any excess marinade. Place the
   vegetables under the grill for 5–10 minutes or until they are
   golden and cooked, but still with a little bite. Transfer to a bowl,
   then set aside and keep warm.

4 Grease the baking sheet with a little of the garlic butter. Arrange
   the prawns on top and spread each one with the remaining butter.
   Season with salt and pepper. Grill the prawns for 5–8 minutes
   until they turn pink and are cooked through.

5 Arrange the vegetables and prawns on a platter. Squeeze over the
   lemon juice and sprinkle with thyme leaves. Serve warm, with
   lemon wedges and some crusty bread.

Seafood risotto

A risotto is such a warming, hearty dish. This seafood version can be made quickly and is full of flavour.

SERVES 4

500g (1lb 2oz) mussels, shell on
200ml (7fl oz) white wine
2 tbsp olive oil
1 large onion, sliced
2 garlic cloves, crushed
225g (8oz) risotto rice
About 400ml (14fl oz) hot fish or vegetable stock
150g (5oz) raw peeled tiger prawns
100g (4oz) frozen petits pois, defrosted
3 tbsp chopped parsley
Juice of 1 lemon
A knob of butter
Salt and freshly ground black pepper

1 Wash the mussels in cold water, removing any beards, and discard any that are already open.

2 Put the mussels in a large saucepan and pour over the wine. Cover with a lid, bring to the boil and boil for about 3–5 minutes until all the mussels have opened. Discard any that remain closed.

3 Drain the mussels through a colander set over a large bowl, then leave to cool slightly. Reserve 12 mussels in their shells. Remove the remaining mussels from the shells and place them in a small bowl. Strain the cooking liquid into a jug.

4 Heat the oil in a large frying pan. Add the onions and fry for a few minutes, then add the garlic and fry for another 10 seconds. Add the rice and stir to coat the grains. Start adding the reserved liquid and stock, a little at a time, waiting until each addition has been absorbed before adding the next. Keep stirring all the time and continue adding stock until the rice is nearly cooked.

5 Add the prawns and peas and stir until the grey prawns have turned pink and are cooked through. Add the shelled mussels, 2 tablespoons of the parsley, the lemon juice and butter, then season with salt and pepper.

6 Stir well, cover the pan with a lid and leave the risotto to stand for a few minutes before serving. Spoon it into a large bowl, arrange the reserved mussels in their shells on top and sprinkle with the remaining chopped parsley.

Roasting tin Thai salmon & vegetables

Packed with Thai flavours and healthy too, this dish has become a firm favourite of mine. And it's so easy to make, as the salmon, sauce and vegetables are all cooked together in one roasting tin in the oven. Thai basil is ideal here but if you don't have any, coriander works well too.

SERVES 6

400ml (14fl oz) tin of full-fat coconut milk
2 tbsp red Thai paste
1 fresh red chilli, deseeded and finely diced
1 large garlic clove, crushed
6cm (2½in) knob of fresh root ginger, coarsely grated
Juice of 2 limes
2 tsp fish sauce
1 cauliflower, split into very small florets
2 Romano peppers, deseeded and cut into large pieces
3 banana shallots, halved
2 tbsp olive oil
1 tbsp runny honey
150g (5oz) baby courgettes, sliced thinly on the diagonal
6 thin salmon fillets (about 150g/5oz each), skinned
Thai basil or coriander, chopped
Salt and freshly ground black pepper

PREPARE AHEAD
Sauce can be made up to 8 hours ahead and the dish assembled when it's time to cook.

1 Preheat the oven to 220°C/200°C fan/Gas 7.

2 Measure the coconut milk, Thai paste, chilli, garlic, ginger, lime juice and fish sauce into a small bowl. Mix well and season with salt and pepper.

3 Scatter the cauliflower florets, peppers and shallots into a large roasting tin or an ovenproof dish. Add a tablespoon of the oil and mix well, then pour over half the sauce, season and drizzle over the honey. Roast in the oven for about 12–15 minutes until the vegetables are starting to brown.

4 Toss the courgettes in the remaining oil and add them and the salmon to the tin. Spoon over the remaining sauce, then roast for a further 10 minutes until the salmon flesh is opaque pink and is just cooked.

5 Sprinkle over the Thai basil or coriander and serve with some steamed rice.

Salmon & fennel one-pot wonder

So easy to make, yet impressive, this is a really healthy meal for the family.
If you're not keen on fennel you could use a thinly sliced medium leek instead,
and you could also replace the salmon with pink trout.

SERVES 4

A large knob of butter
3 large banana shallots, sliced
1 fennel bulb, core removed, thinly sliced
150ml (5fl oz) white wine
200ml (7fl oz) full-fat crème fraîche
4 x 125g (4½oz) thin, centre-cut salmon fillets, skinned, each cut in half lengthways to make 8 thin strips
100g (4oz) frozen petits pois, defrosted
A squeeze of fresh lemon juice
2 tbsp chopped parsley
Salt and freshly ground black pepper

1 Melt the butter in a large, wide-based pan over a gentle heat. Add the shallots and fennel and fry over a high heat for about 2–3 minutes. Lower the heat, cover the pan with a lid and continue to cook for about 8–10 minutes until tender.

2 Pour in the wine and boil to reduce by half, then stir in the crème fraîche and bring to the boil. Season with salt and pepper, then place the salmon strips in a single layer in the sauce. Cover the pan and simmer gently for about 4 minutes until the salmon is nearly cooked.

3 Add the peas, pushing them under the sauce, and continue to cook for about 3 minutes. Stir in the lemon juice, check the seasoning and sprinkle with parsley. Serve with the sauce and some rice, mashed potato, grains or crusty bread.

Haddock & shrimp feast

A good one-pot dish, this is simple to make. It's lovely served in individual bowls, simply garnished with green leaves, and it can be eaten just with a fork, so it's ideal for a party.

SERVES 4

A knob of butter
1 tbsp sunflower oil
2 onions, chopped
2 celery sticks, finely sliced
1 garlic clove, crushed
150g (150g) chestnut mushrooms, thickly sliced
225g (8oz) long-grain rice
200ml (7fl oz) white wine
600ml (1 pint) hot vegetable stock
4 x 125g (4½oz) haddock fillets, skinned weight
150g (5oz) baby spinach leaves
Juice of 1 small lemon
2 tbsp chopped dill
2 tbsp chopped parsley
100ml (3½fl oz) pouring double cream
2 x 50g (2oz) pots of potted shrimp
Salt and freshly ground black pepper

1 You will need a deep flameproof and ovenproof casserole dish, with a lid, that is wide enough for the haddock pieces to sit side by side. Preheat the oven to 180°C/160°C fan/Gas 4.

2 Heat the butter and oil in the casserole dish. Add the onions and celery and fry for about 10 minutes over a medium heat. Then add the garlic and mushrooms and fry for 2 minutes. Add the rice and stir to coat it in the vegetable juices, then fry for a couple more minutes. Pour over the wine and hot stock, then season and bring to the boil. Do not stir the rice.

3 Transfer the dish, uncovered, to the oven and cook for about 15 minutes. Season the pieces of fish and sit them on top of the rice – do not overlap the fillets. Bake for another 8–10 minutes until the fish is just done, then transfer the fish to a warm plate.

4 Add the spinach to the casserole dish and place it on the hob. Cover with a lid and cook for a few minutes until the spinach has just wilted. Remove the lid and stir, then add the lemon juice, herbs and cream. Stir again and check the seasoning.

5 Warm the potted shrimp in a saucepan until the butter has melted. Return the haddock to the pan, spoon the shrimp over the haddock and serve piping hot.

Thai cod cakes with Thai basil & lime sauce

Fishcakes are so popular, and a hint of Thai flavours makes these a great change from the classic version. If you don't have Thai basil, use ordinary basil instead.

MAKES 6

250g (9oz) cod fillet, skinned
and diced
5 spring onions, finely chopped
Finely grated zest of 1 lime
1 garlic clove, crushed
5cm (2in) knob of fresh root
ginger, finely grated
2 tsp red Thai paste
100g (4oz) panko breadcrumbs
1 egg yolk
1 tsp fish sauce
1½ tsp sweet chilli sauce
1 tbsp chopped Thai basil
1 tbsp olive oil
Salt and freshly ground black
pepper

FOR THE LIME & BASIL SAUCE
1 tsp red Thai paste
200g (7oz) full-fat crème fraîche
½ tsp Dijon mustard
2 tbsp snipped chives
2 tbsp chopped Thai basil,
Lime juice, to taste (from the
zested lime above)

PREPARE AHEAD
*Can be made and fried up to
8 hours ahead, then baked in
the oven to serve.*

FREEZE
These freeze well raw.

1   Preheat the oven to 200°C/180°C fan/Gas 6.

2   Put the cod in a food processor with the spring onions, lime zest, garlic, ginger and Thai paste. Whizz for a few seconds until very roughly chopped. Reserve 25g (1oz) of the breadcrumbs, then add the remainder to the processor with the egg yolk, fish sauce, chilli sauce and basil. Season with salt and pepper, then briefly process until the mixture is combined but still has some texture and is not too soft.

3   Divide the mixture into 6 piles. Wet your hands and shape into 6 small flat fishcakes, about 2cm (¾in) thick. Coat them evenly all over in the reserved breadcrumbs.

4   Heat the oil in a small frying pan and fry the cod cakes until browned on both sides. Transfer to a baking sheet and bake in the oven for about 15–20 minutes until cooked through.

5   To make the lime and basil sauce, measure all the ingredients into a bowl and season well to taste. Stir until combined. Serve the cod cakes piping hot, with a dollop of sauce on the side and a watercress salad.

Whole stuffed baked trout with caper butter

Comforting memories create comforting food. Our son Thomas loves fishing, and one of the very first fish he caught, when he was about ten years old, was a sea trout. He was so very proud and we cooked the fish fresh from the sea. This recipe also works well with sea bass.

SERVES 4

2 small to medium pink trout, gutted, cleaned and oven ready
Parsley stalks
1 lemon, thinly sliced
Olive oil, for drizzling
Salt and freshly ground black pepper

FOR THE CAPER BUTTER
25g (1oz) butter, softened
1 tbsp chopped capers
1 tbsp chopped parsley
1 tbsp chopped chives
Zest of ½ lemon

PREPARE AHEAD
Can be prepared, ready for the oven, 6 hours ahead.

1 Preheat the oven to 200°C/180°C fan/Gas 6. Line a large baking sheet with baking paper.

2 To make the caper butter, measure the butter into a bowl, add the capers, herbs, lemon zest and seasoning and mash with a fork.

3 Make 3 equal slashes in one side of each trout and fill the slashes with caper butter. Fill the bellies of the fish with parsley stalks and slices of lemon

4 Place the fish on the baking sheet. Season with salt and pepper and drizzle with a little oil. Bake the fish for about 15–20 minutes until the flesh has turned opaque pink and is just cooked. Remove and leave to rest for a few minutes.

5 Peel off the skin and carefully lift each fillet off the bone. Serve warm in large pieces with any remaining caper butter spooned over, and with green vegetables and new potatoes or salad.

Salmon fillets with cauliflower cheese topping

Salmon fillet is an easy fish to cook but needs a little extra something to make it exciting, so try this cauliflower cheese topping. It gives a lovely flavour and adds texture. Choose thin salmon fillets, cut from the centre of the side of salmon.

SERVES 6

250g (9oz) cauliflower
100g (4oz) full-fat cream cheese
25g (1oz) mature Cheddar
  cheese, grated
50g (2oz) Parmesan cheese,
  grated
2 tsp Dijon mustard
6 x 125g (4½oz) salmon fillets,
  skinned
Juice of ½ large lemon
Paprika, for dusting
Salt and freshly ground black
  pepper

PREPARE AHEAD
*Can be assembled up to 6 hours
ahead.*

1 Preheat the oven to 200°C/180°C fan/Gas 6. Line a baking sheet with baking paper.

2 Break the cauliflower into florets, then whizz them in a processor until they look like couscous. Tip into a bowl and stir in the cream cheese, Cheddar, half the Parmesan, the mustard and lots of salt and pepper. Mix well until combined.

3 Sit the salmon fillets on the baking sheet. Season them on both sides and squeeze over the lemon juice. Divide the topping into 6 portions and spoon over the top of each fillet, using a teaspoon to spread it out to the edges. Sprinkle with the remaining Parmesan and dust with paprika.

4 Bake in the oven for about 15 minutes until the fish is just cooked through and the cauliflower topping is lightly golden. Serve hot, with green vegetables.

Cod goujons with caper herb dip

Think fish fingers or fish and chips – many people's favourite comfort foods.
This is our fresher, lighter version, with no deep-fat frying.

SERVES ABOUT 4
(4 GOUJONS EACH)

50g (2oz) panko breadcrumbs,
  crushed into fine crumbs
1 tbsp finely chopped parsley
Finely grated zest of ½ lemon
25g (1oz) plain flour
2 eggs, beaten
500g (1lb 2oz) cod loin fillet,
  skinned
A little sunflower oil, for frying
Salt and freshly ground black
  pepper

FOR THE CAPER HERB DIP

4 tbsp full-fat mayonnaise
2 tbsp crème fraîche
Juice of ½ lemon
1 tbsp finely chopped parsley
1 tbsp chopped capers
2 tbsp chopped gherkins

PREPARE AHEAD

*Dip can be made up to 3 days
ahead. Goujons can be breaded
up to 6 hours ahead and kept in
the fridge until ready to cook.*

1 Put the breadcrumbs, parsley and lemon zest into a bowl and season with salt and pepper. Stir together to combine.

2 Take three plates. Tip the flour on to one plate and sprinkle with salt and pepper. Pour the beaten egg on to the next plate and scatter the breadcrumbs over the final plate.

3 Put the cod on a board and slice into about 16 goujons measuring about 7.5 x 2.5cm (3 x 1in) thick.

4 Dip the goujons into the flour, making sure they are coated with a thin layer all over. Then dip them into the beaten egg and lastly into the herby panko crumbs.

5 Heat a thin layer of sunflower oil in a large frying pan. When hot, add half the goujons and fry them over a medium heat for about 5 minutes until golden and cooked through. Remove to a plate lined with kitchen paper, then fry the remaining goujons.

6 Measure all the dip ingredients into a small bowl. Season with salt and pepper and mix to combine.

7 Serve the goujons with the dip, a wedge of lemon and skinny sweet potato fries (see page 201).

Glorious fish pie

No book of comfort food would be complete without a fish pie. This is one my family love.

SERVES 6–8

100g (4oz) butter
2 small leeks, thinly sliced
100g (4oz) plain flour
900ml (1½ pints) hot milk
100g (4oz) full-fat crème fraîche
Juice of ½ lemon
Small bunch of dill, chopped
25g (1oz) Parmesan cheese,
　grated
500g (1lb 2oz) fresh haddock,
　skinned and cut into chunks
500g (1lb 2oz) undyed smoked
　haddock, skinned and cut
　into chunks
4 eggs, hard-boiled, peeled and
　quartered

TOPPING
1kg (2lb 3oz) potatoes, peeled
　and cut into even-sized cubes
2 tbsp milk
2 knobs of butter
Salt and freshly ground black
　pepper

PREPARE AHEAD
*Can be made and assembled
up to 8 hours ahead.*

FREEZE
*Freezes well uncooked, without
the eggs, for up to 3 weeks.*

1   You will need a 2.5-litre (4½-pint) ovenproof dish. Preheat the oven to 200°C/180°C fan/Gas 6.

2   Melt the butter in a deep, wide saucepan, add the leeks and cook until softened. Stir in the flour and whisk over the heat for a minute. Blend in the hot milk, whisking until you have a smooth, thick sauce, then simmer for a few minutes.

3   Stir in the crème fraîche, lemon juice, dill and cheese, season with salt and pepper and stir. Remove the sauce from the heat and stir in the fish, then spoon everything into the dish. Push the egg quarters into the mixture, so they are submerged in the sauce, and allow to cool.

4   Put the potatoes in a large pan of cold salted water and bring to the boil. Boil for about 15 minutes until tender, then drain well and return to the pan. Add the milk and a knob of butter, season and mash well.

5   Spoon the mash on top of the fish, spread it out and run a fork over the surface to make a nice pattern. Dot the remaining butter on top of the pie.

6   Bake in the hot oven for about 30–35 minutes until bubbling and golden on top.

Pork, Beef & Lamb

Spicy sausage rolls

Lizzy, our publisher, asked for sausage rolls to be included in the book, as she feels they are among the most comforting of all foods. She's right! If you can't find ready-rolled puff pastry, buy an all-butter 500g (1lb 2oz) block and use about four-fifths.

MAKES 6 MEDIUM
SAUSAGE ROLLS

6 fat pork sausages
2 tbsp sun-dried tomato paste
6 mild peppadew peppers,
    finely chopped
Small bunch of parsley, chopped
1 garlic clove, crushed
1 x 375g (13oz) sheet of ready-
    rolled puff pastry
Flour, for dusting
1 egg, beaten
Salt and freshly ground black
    pepper

PREPARE AHEAD
*Can be made up to 12 hours ahead,
then cook to serve. Or cook up to a
day ahead and reheat to serve.*

FREEZE
*Freeze unbaked. Thaw before
baking.*

1   You will need a large baking sheet. Preheat the oven to 220°C/200°C fan/Gas 7 and line the baking sheet with some non-stick baking paper.

2   To make the filling, remove the sausage meat from the skins and place in a mixing bowl. Add the tomato paste, peppadew peppers, parsley and garlic. Season well and mix with your hands until all is evenly combined.

3   Unroll the pastry and place it on a lightly floured work surface. Roll out the pastry to a slightly bigger rectangle measuring about 40 x 30cm (16 x 12in). Brush the pastry with beaten egg.

4   Divide the sausage mixture into three. Take one portion and roll it into a long sausage shape. Place it lengthways on the pastry, about 10cm (4in) in from the shorter edge. Fold over the pastry to encase the sausage meat and press to seal. Trim the pastry edges to make a long sausage roll, then slice in half to make 2 long sausage rolls measuring about 12cm (5in) long. Fork the edges. Repeat the process twice using the remaining pastry and sausage mixture.

5   Arrange the sausage rolls on the baking sheet and brush with beaten egg. Bake in the oven for 25–30 minutes until golden brown and cooked through in the middle. Serve warm, with tomato ketchup.

Baked pasta lasagne rolls

A great pasta bake, this has rolled pasta sheets filled with sausage meat and spinach, all baked in a tomato sauce. The pasta will be soft underneath and crispy on top.

SERVES 6

6 sheets of fresh lasagne

FOR THE TOMATO SAUCE
2 tbsp olive oil
1 large onion, finely chopped
2 celery sticks, finely diced
1 large garlic clove, crushed
2 x 400g (14oz) tins of chopped
   tomatoes
2 tbsp sun-dried tomato paste
½ tsp sugar
Small bunch of basil, chopped
Salt and freshly ground black
   pepper

FOR THE FILLING
1 tbsp olive oil
300g (11oz) pork sausage meat
1 small fresh red chilli, deseeded
   and finely chopped
150g (5oz) button mushrooms,
   diced
1 garlic clove, crushed
100g (4oz) baby spinach,
   chopped
100ml (3½fl oz) double cream
50g (2oz) Parmesan cheese,
   grated

FOR THE TOPPING
25g (1oz) Gruyère cheese, grated

PREPARE AHEAD
*Can be assembled up to 8 hours
ahead, ready to put in the oven.*

1 You will need a 2–2.25-litre (3½–4-pint) shallow flameproof and ovenproof casserole dish with a lid. Preheat the oven to 200°C/180°C fan/Gas 6.

2 First make the tomato sauce. Heat the oil in the casserole dish, add the onion and celery and fry for a few minutes over a high heat. Add the garlic and fry for 10 seconds. Add the tomatoes, 150ml (5fl oz) of water and the tomato paste, then bring to the boil, stirring. Season and add the sugar, then cover and simmer for about 15 minutes. Add the basil and stir. Spoon 6 heaped tablespoons of tomato sauce into a bowl and set aside.

3 For the filling, heat the oil in a large frying pan. Add the sausage meat and brown it over high heat, breaking it up with a wooden spoon. Add the chilli, mushrooms and garlic and fry for a few minutes, then add the spinach and stir until wilted. Add the cream, then remove the pan from the heat and set aside until the filling is cold. Stir in the Parmesan cheese and season.

4 Soak the lasagne sheets in a dish of boiling water for 2 minutes to soften a little, then drain and pat them dry with kitchen towel. Arrange the lasagne sheets on a work surface and divide the filling mixture between them, spreading it over the sheets. Roll up each one, starting from the short end to make a tight roll, and trim any excess pasta. Slice each tube into 3 pieces, using a sharp knife.

5 Place the swirls, cut side up, in the tomato sauce in the pan, arranging them in a nice pattern. Bake for about 20 minutes until the pasta is just soft and the tomato sauce is bubbling.

6 Remove the dish from the oven, spoon over the reserved tomato sauce and sprinkle with the Gruyère cheese. Put the dish back into the oven for another 10 minutes until the top is crisp. Serve piping hot, with salad.

Swedish meatballs with enriched apple & thyme sauce

Italian meatballs are often served with a tomato sauce and pasta but these have a creamy sauce, as often served in Scandinavia. We think they're best with mash or rice.

SERVES 6

500g (1lb 2oz) minced pork
1 small onion, finely chopped
1 tbsp thyme leaves, finely
  chopped
Finely grated zest of ½ lemon
6 cream crackers, very finely
  crushed
Plain flour, to coat
Olive oil, for frying
Salt and freshly ground black
  pepper

FOR THE SAUCE
A knob of butter
1 small onion, finely chopped
1 dessert apple, finely diced
2 tbsp brandy
300ml (10fl oz) chicken stock
175ml (6fl oz) double cream
A squeeze of lemon juice to taste
2 tsp chopped thyme

PREPARE AHEAD
Raw meatballs can be made up to a day ahead. Can be cooked up to 8 hours ahead and reheated in the hot sauce. Sauce can be made up to 8 hours ahead and thyme added when serving.

FREEZE
Raw meatballs freeze well.

1 Measure all the ingredients for the meatballs, except the flour and oil, into a food processor and season with salt and pepper. Whizz until the mixture is finely chopped but not too smooth, then remove from the processor.

2 Wet your hands – this helps prevent the mixture sticking – and shape the mixture into 30 meatballs. Roll each ball in flour to give a thin coating.

3 Heat a little oil in a large frying pan. Add the meatballs and fry over a medium heat for 8–10 minutes until they are cooked through and golden. Transfer them to a plate.

4 For the sauce, add the butter to the unwashed pan and fry the onion and apple for 5 minutes. Add the brandy, then pour in the stock, bring to the boil and boil for about 2 minutes. Stir in the cream, lemon juice and thyme, season with salt and pepper and simmer until reduced to a coating consistency. Return the meatballs to the pan and heat them through. Serve piping hot.

Sausage & red pepper hot pot

Sausages are one of the most comforting meals – choose your favourites for this recipe. This one-pot stew is a complete main course, with a green vegetable if you like, and will keep all the family happy.

SERVES 4

1 tbsp sunflower oil

8 spicy pork sausages

4 rashers of smoked bacon, finely chopped

1 onion, sliced

1 red pepper, deseeded and cut into large pieces

1 large carrot, diced into small pieces

1 garlic clove, crushed

300ml (10fl oz) chicken stock

400g (14oz) tin of chopped tomatoes

2 tbsp sun-dried tomato paste

2 fresh thyme sprigs

250g (9oz) baby new potatoes, skin on, thickly sliced into discs

Salt and freshly ground black pepper

PREPARE AHEAD
Can be made up to 8 hours ahead. Bring to the boil to reheat.

FREEZE
Freezes well.

1 You will need a large, deep frying pan or sauté pan with a lid or a flameproof casserole dish. Heat the oil in the pan over a high heat. Add the sausages and fry them until browned on all sides, then set them aside. Add the bacon and fry for a few minutes until crisp, then set aside.

2 Add the onion, pepper, carrot and garlic to the pan and fry for 5 minutes over a high heat. Pour in the stock, tomatoes and tomato paste, then add the thyme sprigs. Bring to the boil, add the potatoes and season with salt and pepper.

3 Turn the heat down to a simmer and return the bacon and sausages to the pan. Cover and simmer on the hob for about 20 minutes. Remove the lid and continue to simmer for another 10 minutes until the sauce has reduced a little and the sausages and vegetables are tender. Serve in bowls, with a green vegetable.

Marinated harissa & yoghurt pork kebabs

This blend of spices and yoghurt results in kebabs that are full of flavour. Pork fillet is the most tender of cuts and only needs a short cooking time, so is perfect for kebabs. If you have new wooden skewers, soak them in water before using, then leave them to dry. This will prevent them from burning if you're cooking on a barbecue.

SERVES 4
(2 SKEWERS EACH)

1 pork fillet, trimmed and sliced into 2cm (¾in) pieces
1 red pepper, diced into 2cm (¾in) pieces
Olive oil, for drizzling
Salt and freshly ground black pepper

FOR THE HARISSA MARINADE
Bunch of coriander, chopped
Juice of 1 small lemon and zest of ½
1 small garlic clove, crushed
100g (4oz) Greek yoghurt
1 tsp brown sugar
1 tbsp harissa paste
1 tbsp ground cumin

PREPARE AHEAD
Can be marinated up to a day ahead.

1 You will need 8 skewers, metal or wooden.

2 Measure all the marinade ingredients into a bowl and mix until combined. Add the pork cubes and stir them into the marinade, then season with salt and pepper and stir again. Cover and leave to marinate for 1 hour or overnight.

3 Preheat the grill or barbecue. Thread alternate pieces of pork and pepper on to the skewers, then season and drizzle with oil. If cooking under an indoor grill, place the skewers on a baking sheet lined with foil.

4 Grill the kebabs for about 15 minutes, turning them over halfway through, until brown and cooked. Serve on a platter, with some mixed salad leaves.

Posh bacon, asparagus & mushroom spaghetti

Similar to a carbonara, this will become a go-to special supper dish.
Use pappardelle or tagliatelle instead of spaghetti if you prefer.

SERVES 4

100g (4oz) asparagus spears

200g (7oz) smoked back bacon, chopped into small pieces

1 small leek, finely sliced

A knob of butter

150g (5oz) button mushrooms, sliced

250g (9oz) spaghetti

200ml (7fl oz) pouring double cream

50g (2oz) Parmesan cheese, grated

Juice of ½ lemon

2 tbsp chopped parsley

Salt and freshly ground black pepper

1 Cut the tips off the asparagus spears and slice the stalks on the diagonal into thin pieces.

2 Heat a large frying pan, add the bacon and fry for 4 minutes until crisp. Remove with a slotted spoon and set aside. Add the leek to the pan and fry for 3 minutes. Then add the butter and mushrooms and fry for a few minutes, or until the mushrooms are starting to brown.

3 Meanwhile, cook the pasta in boiling salted water according to the packet instructions, adding the asparagus 3 minutes before the end of the cooking time. Drain, reserving 50ml (2fl oz) of the cooking water.

4 Pour the cream into the frying pan and bring to the boil. Add the spaghetti and asparagus to the pan and toss together. Season and remove the pan from the heat, then add the cheese, lemon and parsley and mix well. Return the bacon to the pan. Add some or all of the reserved water if the sauce is too thick. Serve at once, with a green salad.

Slow-roast hand & spring with crackling & onion gravy

The hand and spring of pork is the upper part of the front leg and is usually sold boned and rolled as a joint. It is less expensive than leg or loin, the major roasting joints. For this recipe, the meat is left on the bone and is braised slowly with onions and herbs until beautifully tender. You can also cook belly of pork this way.

SERVES 8

2 tbsp salt

1 hand and spring pork joint, skin scored

3 large onions, thickly sliced

2 garlic cloves, sliced

8 bay leaves

Small bunch of sage, tied together

700ml (1¼ pints) hot chicken or vegetable stock

25g (1oz) butter

25g (1oz) plain flour

Salt and freshly ground black pepper

1   Preheat the oven to 220°C/200°C fan/Gas 7. Rub salt over the skin of the pork joint. Put the onions, garlic, bay leaves and sage into a small, deep roasting tin, then pour in the stock. Sit the joint on top, skin side up.

2   Cover the whole tray with foil and seal the edges tightly. Place in the oven and roast for about 40 minutes. Reduce the oven temperature to 150°C/130°C fan/Gas 3 and cook for 2½–3 hours, until the meat is very tender and falling off the bone.

3   Transfer the pork to a board. Using a slotted spoon, scoop the onions into a bowl, cover and keep them warm. Remove the bay leaves and sage and discard them. Strain the stock into a jug.

4   Line a baking sheet with foil. Carefully remove the skin from the pork, then snip it into strips with scissors, place on the foil and sprinkle with salt. Cover the pork with foil and keep it warm.

5   Increase the oven temperature to 220°C/200°C fan/Gas 7. Put the baking sheet in the oven and cook the skin for 5–10 minutes until crackled and crisp.

6   Meanwhile, melt the butter in a saucepan. Add the flour and stir over the heat for a few seconds to make a roux. Pour in the hot stock from the pork, whisking until the sauce has thickened. Check the seasoning.

7   Pull the pork off the bone and arrange the meat with the onions on a serving dish. Snip the crackling into pieces and place alongside, then serve with a jug of the hot gravy.

Pork en croute with Stilton & apple

A first-rate dish for a dinner party, this has all the flavours that go well with pork in one lovely bundle.

SERVES 4–6

1 medium egg
1 tbsp olive oil
1 onion, finely chopped
1 dessert apple, peeled and chopped into tiny dice
1 tbsp chopped sage
15g (½oz) panko breadcrumbs
50g (2oz) Stilton cheese, coarsely grated
1 tsp grainy mustard
Large pork fillet, trimmed
375g (13oz) sheet of ready-rolled puff pastry
Plain flour, for dusting
Salt and freshly ground black pepper

FOR THE SAUCE
200ml (7fl oz) white wine
300ml (10fl oz) double cream
50g (2oz) Stilton cheese, grated
1 tsp Dijon mustard
1 tbsp chopped parsley

PREPARE AHEAD
Can be assembled up to 12 hours ahead, ready to roast. Sauce can be made up to a day ahead.

FREEZE
Freezes well raw.

1 You will need a baking sheet lined with baking paper. Reserve a little of the beaten egg in a small bowl to glaze the pastry.

2 Heat a frying pan and add the oil. Fry the onion and apple over a high heat for a few minutes. Lower the heat, cover the pan and leave to cook for about 15 minutes until softened. Remove the pan from the heat, transfer the onion and apple to a bowl and leave to cool. Add the sage, breadcrumbs, Stilton, mustard and the remaining egg to the onion and apple, season well and stir.

3 Place the pork on a board. Cover it with baking paper and bash with a wooden rolling pin in the thickest areas, until the fillet is the same thickness throughout. Keep it in a circular shape. Season the meat and spoon the filling mixture on top, spreading it out to cover the pork fillet completely.

4 Unroll the pastry and lay it on a floured work surface. Roll it out to make a rectangle that is big enough to encase the fillet. Place the pastry on the baking sheet.

5 Put the fillet in the centre of the pastry and brush the pastry around the pork with egg. Slice the pastry extending from the pork into 2cm (¾in) strips. Fold these over to make a plait on top – just like you would plait hair – then trim away any extra leftover pastry. Chill for 30 minutes before cooking.

6 Preheat the oven to 220°c/200°c fan/Gas 7. Brush the plait with egg, then bake for 35–40 minutes. Cover the plait with foil if it is getting too brown. Leave to rest for 10 minutes.

7 Meanwhile, make the sauce. Pour the wine into a large pan and reduce by half over a high heat. Pour in the cream, bring to the boil and reduce a little. Add the Stilton, mustard and season, then stir well, as the cheese may stick to the bottom of the pan. Stir in the parsley just before serving. Carve the pork en croute into thin slices and serve with the sauce and green vegetables.

Orange-glazed ham with mango & orange salsa

Think Christmas and it's family, friends and comforting food for a feast.
A beautiful glazed gammon is a simple but tasty way to serve a great centrepiece.
The gammon can be simmered very slowly on the hob if preferred.

SERVES 8–12

2–3kg (4lb 6oz–6lb 9oz) boned
  smoked gammon joint
1 litre (1¾ pints) orange juice

FOR THE ORANGE GLAZE

100g (4oz) granulated sugar
1 large orange, thinly sliced
  into discs

FOR THE MANGO
& ORANGE SALSA

250g (9oz) peeled mango,
  finely diced
2 oranges, segmented and
  chopped into small pieces
4 tbsp mango chutney
Juice of ½ lemon
3 tbsp chopped parsley
Salt and freshly ground black
  pepper

PREPARE AHEAD
*Can be cooked and glazed up to
3 days ahead and served cold.*

1 Preheat the oven to 150°C/130°C fan/Gas 2.

2 Sit an enamel plate or a small trivet in the base of a deep
   ovenproof pan. The gammon should fit into the pan tightly on
   top of the trivet. Pour in the orange juice and add enough water
   to completely cover the gammon with liquid. Bring to the boil,
   skim the surface, then cover with a lid and transfer to the oven.
   Simmer gently for 20 minutes for every 500g (1lb 2oz). Remove
   from oven and leave to become cold in the cooking liquid.

3 For the orange glaze, put the sugar and 100ml (3½fl oz) of water
   into a saucepan. Stir gently over a low heat until the sugar has
   dissolved, then bring to the boil. Add the thin slices of orange
   to the syrup, then cover and simmer for 10–12 minutes until the
   orange slices are soft but still holding their shape. Lift out the
   orange slices, then continue to boil the syrup over a high heat
   until it has reduced by about half and thickened. Remove from
   the heat and leave to cool. It will thicken further.

4 Line a baking tray or roasting tin with foil and sit the ham on top.
   Remove the skin from the ham and using a sharp knife, score the
   fat. Brush the fat with a little of the syrup. Arrange the orange
   slices in a neat row over the top, then brush with more syrup.
   Preheat the oven to 220°C/200°C fan/Gas 7.

5 Cover the lean meat sides of the gammon with foil to protect the
   ham, but leave the orange-covered top open. Roast in the oven for
   about 30 minutes or until the top is glazed and lightly browned,
   or brown with a blowtorch.

6 To make the salsa, mix all the ingredients together in a bowl and
   season well. Carve the ham and serve with the salsa alongside.

Bolognese bake

This is a Bolognese pasta that can be assembled ahead in one dish, ready to pop in the oven. Frying the mushrooms ensures they keep firm and flavoursome, not soft and soggy.

SERVES 6

1 tbsp olive oil

2 onions, chopped

2 celery sticks, chopped finely

675g (1½lb) minced beef

2 garlic cloves, crushed

2 tbsp tomato purée

2 x 400g (14oz) tins of chopped tomatoes

350ml (12fl oz) beef stock

2 tsp Worcestershire sauce

1 tbsp redcurrant jelly

A knob of butter

250g (9oz) chestnut mushrooms, sliced

1 tbsp chopped fresh thyme leaves

225g (8oz) penne pasta

100g (4oz) mature Cheddar cheese, grated

50g (2oz) Parmesan cheese, grated

Salt and freshly ground black pepper

PREPARE AHEAD
Can be made and assembled ready to cook up to 6 hours ahead.

FREEZE
Freezes well before baking.

1 You will need an ovenproof dish with a capacity of about 1.8 litres (3¼ pints).

2 Heat the oil in a deep frying pan. Add the onions and celery and fry over a high heat for about 3 minutes, until they are beginning to soften. Add the mince and brown quickly, breaking it up with two wooden spoons. Add the garlic and tomato purée and stir for a few seconds.

3 Add the tomatoes, stock, Worcestershire sauce and redcurrant jelly. Stir to combine and season with salt and pepper. Cover and reduce the heat to a low simmer, then simmer for 30–35 minutes.

4 Melt the butter in a frying pan, add the mushrooms and fry them for a minute over a high heat. Put a lid on the pan and cook for 2 minutes to draw out any liquid, then remove the lid and fry for 2 minutes over a high heat to evaporate the liquid. Add the mushrooms and the thyme to the mince, then stir well.

5 Preheat the oven to 160°C/140°C fan/Gas 3. Cook the pasta in boiling salted water according to the packet instructions – keep it al dente. Drain well and run under cold water. Stir the pasta into the mince, then taste to check the seasoning.

6 Spoon everything into the ovenproof dish. Sprinkle with both cheeses and bake in the oven for 25–30 minutes until golden and bubbling around the edges. Serve piping hot, with a green or tomato salad.

Smoky beef casserole with black-eyed beans

This is a warming beef casserole, spiced up with a little chilli and a rich tomato sauce.
The black-eyed beans add heartiness to the dish.

SERVES 6

2 tbsp olive oil

1kg (2lb 3oz) braising beef,
   cut into 2cm (¾in) cubes

2 red onions, thinly sliced

1 green pepper, deseeded and
   diced

3 garlic cloves, crushed

1–2 fresh green chillies,
   deseeded and finely chopped

1 tbsp cumin

2 tsp sweet smoked paprika

400g (14oz) tin of chopped
   tomatoes

350ml (12fl oz) good beef stock

1 tbsp tomato purée

½ tsp light muscovado sugar

2 x 400g (14oz) tins of black-
   eyed beans, drained

Salt and freshly ground black
   pepper

PREPARE AHEAD
Can be made up to 2 days ahead.
Add beans when reheating.

FREEZE
Freezes well without the beans.

1 Preheat the oven to 160°C/140°C fan/Gas 3.

2 Heat the oil in a large sauté pan with a lid or in a flameproof
   and ovenproof casserole dish. Add the beef and brown it over
   a high heat until golden all over. It's best to do this in a couple
   of batches so you don't overcrowd the pan. Remove the beef with
   a slotted spoon and set aside.

3 Add the onions, pepper, garlic and chilli and fry for 3–4 minutes,
   then add the spices and fry for 30 seconds. Add the remaining
   ingredients, except the beans, and bring to the boil, then season
   and stir for a couple of minutes.

4 Put the beef back into the pan. Cover with a lid and transfer to
   the oven for 1½–2 hours until the beef is tender. Stir in the beans
   30 minutes before the end of the cooking time. Serve hot, with a
   variety of fresh vegetables.

Mustard steak with vine tomatoes & foolproof Béarnaise sauce

Steak is both one of the most comforting of meals and simple to cook, so a real treat. Choose the cut you like best – my favourite is fillet. I find that there is no need to clarify the butter for the sauce. Cutting it into softish cubes works well.

SERVES 2

FOR THE FOOLPROOF
BÉARNAISE SAUCE
1 shallot, finely chopped
4 tbsp white wine vinegar
2 egg yolks
100g (4oz) soft butter, cut
   into cubes
1 tsp chopped tarragon
1 tbsp chopped parsley

FOR THE STEAK
1 tsp paprika
1 tsp mustard seeds, crushed
½ tsp celery salt
2 x 150g (5oz) fillet steaks,
   cut from the centre fillet,
   at room temperature
Olive oil, for drizzling
2 vines of cherry tomatoes
Salt and crushed black pepper

PREPARE AHEAD
Can prepare the sauce ahead and keep it warm in a Thermos for up to 2 hours.

1   First make the sauce. Measure the shallot and vinegar into a small pan and add 2 tablespoons of water. Bring to the boil, reduce the liquid to 1 tablespoon, then pour through a sieve into a heatproof bowl. Add the yolks and a little salt, then whisk to combine.

2   Heat a pan of water to a gentle simmer, then sit the bowl with the egg mixture on top. Using a balloon whisk, whisk over the heat, adding a cube of butter at a time until the sauce starts to thicken. Continue whisking until all the butter has been incorporated and the sauce is the consistency of thick mayonnaise. Add the herbs and season. Take care not to let the water boil otherwise the sauce will be too hot and may separate and curdle.

3   For the steak, measure the paprika, mustard seeds and celery salt into a bowl and mix together.

4   Put the steaks on a board. Drizzle them with oil, then season with salt and crushed pepper and sprinkle over half the spices. Rub all this into the steaks, then turn them over and rub the remaining spices on the other side.

5   Heat a frying pan until hot. Add the steaks and fry for about 2 minutes, then turn them over and cook for 2 minutes on the other side. This should give you medium steaks, depending on the thickness. Transfer the steaks to a plate, cover with foil and leave to rest for about 10 minutes.

6   Leave the tomatoes on the vines and add them to the pan. Fry gently for a minute on each side until slightly soft.

7   Serve the steaks with the vine tomatoes, warm Béarnaise sauce and sweet potato skinny fries (see page 201).

Mexican chilli con carne

Chilli con carne is the ultimate in simple comfort dishes – serve up bowls of chilli, rice and toppings and dig in! This is a real crowd pleaser and one all the family love.

SERVES 6

2 tbsp olive oil
2 onions, chopped
1 green pepper, deseeded and chopped
2 garlic cloves, crushed
1–2 fresh red chillies, deseeded and diced
800g (1lb 12oz) lean minced beef
1½ tbsp paprika
1½ tbsp ground cumin
2 x 400g (14oz) tins of chopped tomatoes
2 tbsp tomato purée
200ml (7fl oz) beef stock
1 x 400g (14oz) tin of kidney beans, drained and rinsed
2 tbsp mango chutney
Salt and freshly ground black pepper

TO SERVE
Grated mature Cheddar cheese
Soured cream
Guacamole
Coriander leaves
Lime wedges

PREPARE AHEAD
Can be made up to a day ahead.

FREEZE
Freezes well.

1 You will need a large, deep frying pan or sauté pan with a lid or an ovenproof, flameproof casserole dish. Preheat the oven to 160°C/140°C fan/Gas 3.

2 Heat the oil in the frying pan and fry the onions and pepper for a few minutes over a high heat. Add the garlic and chillies and fry for about 2 minutes. Add the beef and brown with the vegetables, stirring until golden all over.

3 Sprinkle in the paprika and cumin, then stir in the tomatoes, tomato purée and stock. Add the beans and chutney and season with salt and pepper. Cover the pan with a lid and bring to a rolling boil, then transfer to the oven for about 1½ hours or until the meat is tender.

4 Serve hot, with rice and bowls of cheese, soured cream and guacamole to spoon on top. Garnish with coriander leaves and lime wedges.

Cottage pie with a bit of a kick

Made with minced beef and a topping of mashed potato, cottage pie is a family comfort classic. The recipe below can also be made with minced lamb, in which case it is called shepherd's pie. It's best to choose a wide dish rather than a deep one, so everyone has plenty of golden topping. Don't cut the potatoes too small or they can become waterlogged when boiled and make the mash wet. Use hot milk for the mash if time allows.

SERVES 6

1 tbsp sunflower oil
2 large onions, chopped
2 celery sticks, finely diced
1kg (2lb 3oz) lean minced beef
50g (2oz) plain flour
200ml (7fl oz) port
450ml (15fl oz) hot beef stock
1 tbsp tomato purée
2 tsp Worcestershire sauce
4 bay leaves
Salt and freshly ground black pepper

TOPPING

1kg (2lb 3oz) large potatoes, cut into large even-sized cubes
A knob of butter
2 tbsp milk
50g (2oz) mature Cheddar cheese, grated

PREPARE AHEAD
Can be made and assembled up to a day ahead.

FREEZE
Freezes well.

1 You will need a large frying pan or sauté pan with a lid, or a flameproof, ovenproof casserole dish, and a 1.8 litre (3¼ pint) ovenproof dish measuring about 15 x 25 x 5cm (6 x 10 x 2in). Preheat the oven to 160°C/140°C fan/Gas 3.

2 Heat the oil in the pan. Add the onions and celery and fry for a few minutes. Add the mince and brown with the vegetables until the mince is golden. Sprinkle in the flour and fry for 30 seconds. Gradually pour in the port and hot stock and stir until the sauce is smooth.

3 Add the tomato purée, Worcestershire sauce and bay leaves. Season with salt and pepper. Bring to the boil, cover with a lid and transfer to the oven for 1–1½ hours until the meat is tender. Remove the bay leaves and spoon the filling into the ovenproof dish. Leave to cool.

4 Place the potatoes in a pan of cold, salted water and bring to the boil. Cook for about 15 minutes until tender. Drain well, add the butter and milk and mash until smooth.

5 Spoon the mash over the pie filling, carefully spreading it to the edges until all the filling is covered. Sprinkle with the grated cheese.

6 Preheat the oven to 200°C/180°C fan/Gas 6 and bake the pie for about 30–35 minutes until the top is brown and bubbling. Serve piping hot, with green vegetables.

Boeuf Bourguignon

A French classic, this is the ultimate comfort stew, with a warming, intense red wine flavour. The secret is to reduce the red wine first to give a lovely richness to the dish.

SERVES 6

600ml (1 pint) red wine
2 tbsp sunflower oil
900g (2lb) braising beef, cut into 2cm (¾in) cubes
150g (5oz) smoked streaky bacon, chopped into small pieces
500g (1lb 2oz) whole baby shallots, peeled
2 garlic cloves, crushed
45g (1½oz) plain flour
200ml (7fl oz) beef stock
1 tbsp redcurrant jelly
1 tbsp tomato purée
3 bay leaves
1 tbsp chopped thyme leaves
500g (1lb 2oz) small button mushrooms
Salt and freshly ground black pepper

PREPARE AHEAD
Can be made up to a day ahead.

FREEZE
Freezes well. Add mushrooms when reheating.

1 Pour the wine into a saucepan and boil over a high heat until it has reduced to 450ml (15fl oz) – just over one-third.

2 You will need a large frying pan or sauté pan with a lid or a flameproof and ovenproof casserole dish. Preheat the oven to 160°C/140°C fan/Gas 3.

3 Heat the oil in the pan. Add half the beef and brown over a high heat until sealed and golden all over. Remove with a slotted spoon and set aside on a plate. Brown the remaining beef in the same way and set aside.

4 Add the bacon to the pan and fry until crisp. Set aside with the beef. Add the shallots and brown them over a high heat for a few minutes, then add the garlic and stir for a few seconds.

5 Return the beef and bacon to the pan. Sprinkle in the flour, stir to coat the beef and vegetables and then fry for a minute over the heat. Pour in the reduced wine and stock and stir until the sauce has thickened.

6 Add the redcurrant jelly, tomato purée, bay leaves and thyme. Season with salt and pepper and bring to the boil. Cover with a lid and transfer to the preheated oven for about 2 hours. Remove from the oven and stir in the mushrooms. Cover again and return to the oven for a further 30 minutes until the beef is completely tender. Serve piping hot, with mashed potatoes and a favourite green vegetable.

Matchday beef & ale shortcrust pie

An old-fashioned treat and why not? This pie of gently cooked minced beef encased in shortcrust pastry is cooked in a traybake tin so it can be cut into squares.

SERVES 8

1 tbsp sunflower oil
2 onions, finely chopped
3 celery sticks, finely chopped
1 large carrot, finely chopped
800g (1lb 12oz) lean minced beef
50g (2oz) plain flour
300ml (10fl oz) ale
150ml (5fl oz) strong beef stock
1 tbsp Worcestershire sauce
1 tbsp tomato purée
Dash of gravy browning
1 tbsp redcurrant jelly
Salt and freshly ground black pepper

FOR THE SHORTCRUST PASTRY
350g (12oz) strong white flour, plus extra for dusting
100g (4oz) lard, diced
50g (2oz) butter, diced
½ tsp salt
1 egg, beaten

PREPARE AHEAD
Can be made up to a day ahead and reheated.

FREEZE
Cooked pie freezes well.

1 You will need a 36.5 x 26 x 4cm (14½ x 10 x 1¾in) traybake tin and a large frying pan with a lid. Preheat the oven to 160°C/140°C fan/Gas 3.

2 Heat the oil in the frying pan, add the onions, celery and carrot and fry for a few minutes. Add the mince and brown with the vegetables over a high heat. Sprinkle in the flour and stir for a few seconds over the heat, then pour in the ale and stock and stir until smooth. Bring to the boil, add the Worcestershire sauce, tomato purée, gravy browning and redcurrant jelly, then season with salt and pepper. Cover the pan with a lid and transfer to the oven for about 1 hour until tender. Leave to cool.

3 For the pastry, measure the flour, lard, butter and salt into a food processor. Whizz until the mixture resembles breadcrumbs, then add about 150ml (5fl oz) of water and whizz until the mixture comes together into a soft dough. Alternatively, rub the flour, lard and butter together with your fingertips, then add the water.

4 Lightly knead the dough into a ball, then divide into a fraction over one-third and a fraction under two-thirds. Place the larger piece on a floured surface and roll out to a rectangle just larger than the tin. Place the pastry in the tin, line the base and sides and level the edges. Prick the base with a fork.

5 Spoon the cold beef mixture into the tin and level the surface. Brush the edges of the pastry with beaten egg. Roll out the rest of the pastry to the size of the top of the pie and place over the filling. Press all around the edges to seal and cut away any excess. Crimp the edges and brush with beaten egg, then make a hole in the centre with the point of a knife to allow the steam to escape.

6 Preheat the oven to 200°C/180°C fan/Gas 6. Bake the pie for about 40–45 minutes until the pastry is golden and cooked on top and underneath. Serve hot, with green vegetables and mash.

Braised lamb with sweet potato & haricot beans

A hearty family stew, this is full of flavour and perfect for feeding a crowd.
If an extra person turns up unexpectedly, just add another can of drained beans!

SERVES 6

2 tbsp sunflower oil

1kg (2lb 3oz) lamb neck fillet, diced

2 large onions, sliced

4 celery sticks, sliced

1 garlic clove, crushed

1 tbsp cumin powder

1 tbsp medium curry powder

450ml (15fl oz) lamb or beef stock

1 x 400g (14oz) tin of chopped tomatoes

1 tbsp sun-dried tomato purée or paste

2 tbsp mango chutney

1 x 400g (14oz) tin of haricot beans, drained and rinsed

2 sweet potatoes, peeled and sliced into 2cm (¾in) cubes

Salt and freshly ground black pepper

PREPARE AHEAD
Can be made up to 2 days ahead up to the end of step 3. Reheat, then add the beans and potatoes and proceed as above.

1 You will need a large deep frying pan or sauté pan with a lid or a flameproof and ovenproof casserole dish. Preheat the oven to 160°C/140°C fan/Gas 3.

2 Heat a tablespoon of the oil in the pan. Quickly fry the lamb over a high heat, until golden brown all over – you may need to do this in batches so as not to overcrowd the pan. Remove each batch with a slotted spoon and set aside.

3 Add the remaining oil to the same pan and fry the onions, celery and garlic for a few minutes. Add the spices and fry for another 30 seconds, stirring. Add the stock, tomatoes, tomato purée or paste and the mango chutney. Bring to the boil, stirring, then add the lamb and season with salt and pepper. Stir for a few minutes, then cover the pan with a lid and transfer to the oven for about an hour.

4 Put the pan back on the hob and add the beans and sweet potatoes. Bring everything back up to the boil, then cover the pan again and return to the oven. Continue to simmer for a further 45 minutes or until the lamb is tender and the potatoes are just cooked but still holding their shape. Check the seasoning and serve piping hot.

French slow-roast lamb with ratatouille

This all-in-one slow roast with ratatouille-style vegetables is great for feeding a crowd. It does need a long time in the oven, but this means that the lamb is beautifully tender and you have time to pop to the pub or go for a walk!

SERVES 6

Large leg or shoulder of lamb, about 2kg (4lb 6oz), bone in

2 garlic cloves, sliced into slivers

3 onions, thickly sliced

2 red peppers, deseeded and chopped into large pieces

1 large aubergine, chopped into large pieces

1 x 400g (14oz) tin of chopped tomatoes

300ml (10fl oz) beef or chicken stock

2 tbsp sun-dried tomato paste

1 tbsp chopped fresh thyme leaves

3 fresh bay leaves

1 tbsp honey

2 tsp paprika

Salt and freshly ground black pepper

FOR THE RUB

2 tbsp chopped thyme leaves

1 tbsp paprika

2 tbsp olive oil

1 You will need a large, deep roasting tin. Preheat the oven to 220°C/200°C fan/Gas 7.

2 For the rub, put the thyme, paprika and oil in a small bowl, mix well and season. Make holes in the joint of lamb with a small sharp knife and spread the rub all over it. Insert the garlic slivers into the holes and season the lamb with salt and pepper. Put the lamb in a large roasting tin and add the onions around and underneath. Roast in the oven for about 40 minutes.

3 Lower the oven temperature to 160°C/140°C fan/Gas 3. Scatter the peppers and aubergine around the lamb. Pour the tomatoes into a bowl, add the stock, sun-dried tomato paste, thyme, bay leaves and honey, then stir to combine. Pour all this into the roasting tin over the peppers and aubergine and stir, then sprinkle the paprika over the vegetables.

4 Cover the whole tin with foil and return to the oven to roast for about 4 hours until the lamb is tender and falling off the bone.

5 Shred the meat or carve into slices. Drain any fat from the top of the sauce and serve with the ratatouille vegetables alongside.

Rack of lamb with garlic minted potatoes

An elegant dish but also so comforting and just right for a smart occasion.
The port gravy adds a gentle richness and the garlic potatoes are rustic
and simple. Each rack of lamb has seven chops.

SERVES 4–6

2 tbsp olive oil, plus 2 tsp

1kg (2lb 3oz) potatoes, such
 as Maris Pipers, diced into
 1cm (½in) cubes

1 tsp honey

1 tsp paprika

2 small well-trimmed racks
 of lamb

1 garlic clove, crushed

1 tbsp finely chopped fresh
 mint

Salt and freshly ground black
 pepper

FOR THE GRAVY

25g (1oz) butter

3 tbsp flour

100ml (3½fl oz) port

350ml (12fl oz) hot well-
 flavoured beef or lamb stock

1 tbsp redcurrant jelly

PREPARE AHEAD
*Gravy can be made up to 2 days
ahead and the meat juices added
after roasting. Lamb can be
browned up to 6 hours ahead,
ready for the oven.*

FREEZE
Gravy freezes well.

1 Preheat the oven to 220°C/200°C fan/Gas 7. Pour the
 2 tablespoons of oil into a large roasting tin and place in
 the oven until hot.

2 Add the potatoes to the tin, season and turn in the hot oil.
 Return to the oven for about 10–15 minutes until the potatoes
 are very lightly golden.

3 Measure the honey, paprika and the remaining 2 teaspoons of oil
 into a bowl and mix together to make a paste. Spread this over
 the skin side of the lamb. Heat a frying pan until hot and brown
 the racks until sealed on all sides, but still raw in the middle.

4 Arrange the lamb in the centre of the roasting tin, pushing the
 potatoes around the edges, and roast for about 15–17 minutes
 until the meat is cooked but still pink.

5 Remove the lamb and set it aside to rest. Add the garlic to the
 potatoes, season with salt and toss together. Return to the oven
 for a further 2 minutes. Remove from the oven and sprinkle over
 the chopped mint.

6 To make the gravy, melt the butter in a saucepan. Add the flour
 and whisk over the heat for 10 seconds. Pour in the port and
 stock and whisk together until smooth. Reduce over the heat to
 a thin sauce consistency. Add the jelly and seasoning and pour
 in any lamb juices from the resting lamb. Whisk to combine and
 pour into a jug.

7 Carve the lamb into chops and serve with the garlic minted
 potatoes and the gravy.

Mustard kidneys

This is an old-fashioned dish but I love it and it reminds me of my parents when I was growing up. Mum would have made a boring meat gravy, but this creamy wine sauce makes it such a comforting meal. It's quick and simple to cook too. It is important to remove the inedible core from each kidney.

SERVES 2

350g (12oz) lamb's kidneys, skinned, cored and sliced in half
Plain flour, to coat
1 tbsp oil
A knob of butter
1 onion, finely chopped
150ml (5fl oz) white wine
150ml (5fl oz) pouring double cream
1 tbsp grainy mustard
2 tsp Dijon mustard
½ tsp sugar
2 tbsp chopped parsley
Salt and freshly ground black pepper

1 Season the kidneys and toss them in flour until thinly coated.

2 Heat a large frying pan over a high heat, then add the oil and butter. When the butter is foaming, add the kidneys and fry for 1–2 minutes on each side until golden and just cooked in the middle. Set aside.

3 Add the onion to the unwashed pan and fry for a couple of minutes. Cover the pan with a lid and leave the onion to cook over a low heat for about 5 minutes until softened.

4 Add the wine, turn the heat up to high and boil until the wine has reduced by half. Pour in the cream and boil for another few minutes. Then add the mustards and sugar and season with salt and pepper.

5 Return the kidneys and any juices to the pan and toss them in the sauce to coat. Sprinkle with chopped parsley and serve immediately, with rice.

Vegetable Mains

Veggie burgers

Healthy and hearty, these are bursting with flavour and goodness. We find that baby spinach is more tender than large leaves, but if you grow your own, just finely shred the larger leaves.

MAKES 6 BURGERS

1 tbsp olive oil

1 large onion, finely chopped

1 garlic clove, crushed

75g (3oz) baby spinach

1 x 400g (14oz) tin of
   butterbeans, drained

1 x 400g (14oz) tin of kidney
   beans, drained

Small bunch of basil, chopped

8 sun-dried tomatoes, chopped

50g (2oz) Parmesan cheese,
   finely grated

FOR THE COATING

About 50g (2oz) plain flour

2 tbsp olive oil

PREPARE AHEAD

*Can be made up to a day ahead,
ready to fry just before serving.*

1 Heat the olive oil in a frying pan. Add the onion and fry for few minutes over a high heat. Stir in the garlic, cover the pan and lower the heat. Cook for about 15 minutes until the onion is soft. Remove the lid, turn up the heat and fry the spinach until wilted. Spoon everything into a bowl and set aside to cool.

2 Put the beans, basil, tomatoes, cheese and cold spinach mixture into a food processor. Quickly pulse until roughly chopped and season well. Do not over whizz – the mixture should still have some texture. Shape into 6 equal-sized burgers and chill in the fridge for 30 minutes.

3 When ready to serve, spread the flour on a plate and coat the burgers with flour. Heat the oil in a large frying pan and fry the burgers for about 3 minutes on each side until golden brown and heated through. Serve hot, with salad.

Mac 'n' cheese

The ultimate comfort food dish, this is one that shouldn't be messed with!
Perfect for a family with a gang of teenagers and their friends to feed. You might
think you have too much sauce for the amount of pasta, but it will be fine.

SERVES 4-6

200g (7oz) macaroni
50g (2oz) butter
50g (2oz) flour
900ml (1½ pints) hot milk
1 tbsp Dijon mustard
75g (3oz) Parmesan cheese,
    grated
75g (3oz) Cheddar cheese,
    grated
Salt and freshly ground black
    pepper

PREPARE AHEAD
*Can be assembled up to 6 hours
ahead. Cook in a preheated oven,
180°C/160°C fan/Gas 4, for about
25 minutes.*

FREEZE
*Can be frozen uncooked. Preheat the
oven to 180°C/160°C fan/Gas 4 and
cook from frozen for 30–40 minutes.*

1   You will need a 2.5-litre (4½-pint) ovenproof dish. Cook the pasta
    in boiling salted water according to the packet instructions. Drain
    and set aside.

2   Melt the butter in a saucepan, add the flour and whisk over the
    heat for 30 seconds to make a roux. Whisk in the hot milk, a little
    at a time, to make a smooth sauce. Continue to whisk until the
    sauce is boiling and has thickened. Remove the pan from the heat
    and add the mustard, seasoning and three-quarters of the cheese.

3   Preheat the grill to high. Add the cooked pasta to the hot sauce,
    stir and pour everything into an ovenproof dish. Sprinkle over the
    remaining cheese. Place the dish under the hot grill for about
    5-10 minutes until the top is golden and bubbling.

Orzo salad with grilled vegetables & olives

Orzo is a versatile pasta and one of the few types I'm happy to eat cold,
as it is very small. The roasted vegetables are vibrant and tasty.

SERVES 4

150g (5oz) orzo pasta

1 red pepper, deseeded and
   sliced into chunks

1 courgette, sliced into thick
   rounds

1 aubergine, halved and sliced

3 tbsp olive oil

100g (4oz) pitted dry black
   olives, sliced

100g (4oz) cherry tomatoes,
   sliced in half and into thin
   slices

Salt and freshly ground black
   pepper

FOR THE LEMON HERB
DRESSING

6 tbsp olive oil

1 tbsp balsamic vinegar

2 tbsp white wine vinegar

1 tsp sugar

Juice of ½ small lemon

1 bunch of dill, chopped

1 bunch of basil, chopped

1 shallot, sliced

1 garlic clove, crushed

PREPARE AHEAD
*Can be prepared up to 6 hours
ahead, then tossed in the dressing
up to an hour ahead.*

1   Cook the orzo until tender according to the packet instructions,
    drain and run under cold water. Preheat the grill to high.

2   Arrange the pieces of pepper, courgette and aubergine on a large
    baking sheet in a single layer. Brush with the oil and season with
    salt and pepper. Place under the grill for about 5 minutes until
    charred, turning once. You may need to do this in batches. Set
    aside to cool.

3   To make the dressing mix all the ingredients together in a large
    bowl. Add the orzo and stir, then add the vegetables, olives and
    tomatoes. Season well and serve cold or warm.

Penne pasta with peppers, garlic mushrooms & asparagus

Pasta is such a family favourite. We particularly love penne, as it is easy to eat with just a fork and easy to serve too.

SERVES 4–6

250g (9oz) penne pasta

400g (14oz) asparagus spears, tips removed and stems sliced into rings

1 tbsp olive oil

1 large red pepper, deseeded and diced

200g (7oz) button mushrooms, halved

1 garlic clove, crushed

200ml (7oz) pouring double cream

1 tbsp chopped thyme leaves

75g (3oz) Parmesan cheese, grated

Juice of ½ small lemon

Salt and freshly ground black pepper

1 Cook the pasta in boiling salted water according to the packet instructions. Add the asparagus tips and rings 3 minutes before the end of the cooking time. Drain the pasta and asparagus and set aside.

2 Meanwhile, heat the oil in a large frying pan. Add the pepper and fry for 3 minutes, then add the mushrooms and fry for another minute. Cover the pan with a lid and leave to cook for 2 minutes. Remove the lid and cook over a high heat to evaporate any liquid, then cook for another minute until the mushrooms are lightly browned. Add the garlic and fry for a few seconds, then add the cream and thyme. Bring to the boil and season well.

3 Drain the pasta and asparagus and add them to the sauce. Add the cheese and lemon juice, then toss together and check the seasoning. Serve piping hot, in bowls.

Mushroom, lentil & double potato jumble

A hearty meat-free dish, this is just right for feeding a gang of hungry people.
It's served in one dish and can be prepared ahead, ready to pop in the oven when it's
nearly time to eat. And it's so full of flavour the carnivores won't miss their meat!

SERVES 6

2 tbsp olive oil
2 onions, roughly chopped
1 garlic clove, crushed
175g (6oz) dried Puy lentils
150ml (5fl oz) white wine
1½ tbsp sun-dried tomato paste
600ml (1 pint) vegetable stock
8 sun-dried tomatoes, chopped
1½ tbsp Worcestershire sauce
25g (1oz) butter, plus extra for
    greasing
500g (1lb 2oz) chestnut
    mushrooms, sliced
Salt and freshly ground black
    pepper

FOR THE TOPPING

350g (12oz) sweet potatoes,
    peeled and diced into 2cm
    (¾in) cubes
350g (12oz) white potatoes,
    peeled and diced into 2cm
    (¾in) cubes
A knob of butter
1 garlic clove, crushed
2 tbsp snipped chives
50g (2oz) mature Cheddar
    cheese, grated

PREPARE AHEAD
*Can be made up to a day ahead, up
to the final 20 minutes of baking
with the topping.*

1   You will need an ovenproof dish with a capacity of about 1.8 litres
    (3¼ pints) and measuring about 15 x 25 x 5cm (6 x 10 x 2in). You
    will also need an ovenproof frying pan or sauté pan with a lid.
    Preheat the oven to 180°C/160°C fan/Gas 4 and butter the dish.

2   Heat the oil in the frying pan, add the onions and fry for about
    5 minutes. Add the garlic and fry for about 10 seconds. Add the
    lentils, white wine, tomato paste and stock, stir and bring to the
    boil. Add the sun-dried tomatoes and season with salt and pepper.
    Cover the pan with a lid and transfer to the oven for about 50–60
    minutes or until the lentils are cooked and the liquid is absorbed.
    Stir in the Worcestershire sauce.

3   Meanwhile, melt the butter in a pan, add the mushrooms and fry
    over a high heat for a minute. Cover with a lid and cook for few
    minutes more over a gentle heat. Remove the lid and increase
    the heat to evaporate the liquid. Season with salt and pepper.
    Add to the lentil mixture, stir and spoon into an ovenproof dish.

4   Increase the oven temperature to 220°C/200°C fan/Gas 7.

5   For the topping, cook the potatoes in a pan of boiling water for
    5–8 minutes until just soft, then drain well. Melt the butter in the
    empty pan, tip the potatoes back in and add the garlic and chives.
    Season with salt and pepper and carefully mix to coat the potatoes
    in the herby, garlicky butter.

6   Spoon the potatoes on top of the lentil mixture and sprinkle with
    the grated cheese. Bake for about 20 minutes until crispy brown
    and bubbling around the edges. Serve piping hot, with some
    green vegetables.

Golden cauliflower steaks with tomato & garlic salsa

My favourite food of the moment is cauliflower steaks, which can be served with lots of different flavours. During cooking, keep the heat to medium and check the cauliflower is golden and not turning too brown. The salsa with a hint of chilli gives the cauliflower a little extra heat and you can add more chilli if you like.

SERVES 4–6

1 large cauliflower
2 tbsp olive oil
2 knobs of butter

FOR THE SALSA

1kg (2lb 3oz) ripe red tomatoes
2 tbsp olive oil
1 onion, chopped
1 small red fresh chilli, deseeded
   and chopped
2 garlic cloves, crushed
100ml (3½fl oz) white wine
2 tbsp tomato purée
½ tsp sugar
Salt and freshly ground black
   pepper

PREPARE AHEAD
*Salsa can be made up to
a day ahead.*

1 First make the salsa. Blanch the tomatoes in a pan of boiling water for 10–15 seconds. Drain and put them into a bowl of cold water. Peel off the skins and deseed the tomatoes. Chop into large dice.

2 Heat the oil in a frying pan. Add the onion and chilli and fry over a medium heat for 5 minutes. Add the garlic and tomatoes and fry for a few minutes, then cover the pan and simmer for 5 minutes. Add the wine and tomato purée, then increase the heat and simmer for a few minutes until the wine has reduced and the tomatoes have broken down, but still retain a little texture. Season well and add the sugar.

3 Cut the cauliflower into slices about 2cm (¾in) thick. Cut each slice in half widthways through the core. Heat a tablespoon of the oil and a knob of butter in a frying pan over a medium heat. Add half the cauliflower steaks and fry for about 4 minutes until golden brown. Turn them over, cover with a lid and fry for 2 minutes, then remove the lid and fry for another 2 minutes. Remove the slices from the pan and keep warm, then repeat with the remaining cauliflower.

4 Serve the hot golden cauliflower steaks with the tomato salsa and a dressed salad.

Sweet potato & spinach pithivier

A pithivier is a round pie, usually made by baking two discs of puff pastry with a filling enclosed between them. The pie should be slightly domed and is traditionally decorated with spiral lines drawn from the centre outwards with the point of a knife and with scalloping on the edge. We buy puff pastry rather than making it, which is a cheat but quicker!

SERVES 4–6

200g (7oz) sweet potato, peeled and diced into 2cm (¾in) pieces
25g (1oz) butter
1 small leek, sliced
1 small onion, sliced
25g (1oz) plain flour, plus extra for dusting
250ml (9fl oz) hot milk
75g (3oz) spinach, coarsely chopped
1 tbsp grainy mustard
50g (2oz) mature Cheddar cheese, grated
1 x 320g (11oz) block of puff pastry
1 egg, beaten
Salt and freshly ground black pepper

PREPARE AHEAD
Can be assembled up to 6 hours ahead and kept in the fridge.

1   You will need a baking sheet lined with non-stick baking paper. Preheat the oven to 220°C/200°C fan/Gas 7.

2   Cook the sweet potato in boiling salted water for about 8 minutes until just soft, then drain.

3   Melt the butter in a wide saucepan. Add the leek and onion and fry them gently for about 5–7 minutes until soft. Add the flour and stir it in over the heat for a minute. Add the milk, a little at a time, stirring until the sauce has thickened. Add the spinach and stir until wilted. Stir in the mustard and cheese and season with salt and pepper, then add the cooked sweet potatoes. Transfer to a bowl, leave to cool, then chill in the fridge until cold.

4   Roll out the pastry on a floured surface until it is very thin. Cut out a 23cm (9 inch) circle and another that is slightly bigger.

5   Put the smaller circle on the lined baking sheet. Spoon the cold mixture into the centre, leaving a 2cm (¾in) border around the edge. Brush the edge with beaten egg. Place the larger circle on top and press the edges to seal. Crimp around the edges and make a small hole in the middle of the pie to let out any steam. Starting from the centre, mark crescent-shaped lines, about 2cm (¾in) apart, down to the edge. Chill the pie in the fridge for 15 minutes if time allows.

6   Brush the pie with the remaining beaten egg and bake for 25–30 minutes until the pastry has puffed up, is cooked through and is crisp on top and underneath. Serve warm, with a dressed salad.

Onion, artichoke & sage open tart

With buttery puff pastry and a deliciously herby filling, this tart is simple to make and so good to eat. Puff is the ultimate comfort food pastry and works so well with these vegetables. You can buy chargrilled artichokes but they are often packed in oil, so drain them well before adding them to the tart.

SERVES 6

4 tbsp olive oil
4 large onion, sliced into thick wedges
1 tsp light brown sugar
1 tsp balsamic vinegar
400g (14oz) mixed mushrooms (such as chestnut, shiitake, button), thickly sliced
1 x 375g (13oz) sheet of ready-rolled puff pastry
1 large egg, beaten
75ml (3fl oz) pouring double cream
2 tsp chopped sage
1 tsp chopped thyme leaves
100g (4oz) mature Cheddar cheese, grated
175g (6oz) chargrilled artichokes, drained and cut into large pieces
Salt and freshly ground black pepper

PREPARE AHEAD
Can be assembled up to 4 hours ahead, ready to put in the oven.

1   You will need a large baking sheet lined with non-stick baking paper. Preheat the oven to 220°C/200°C fan/Gas 7.

2   Heat 2 tablespoons of the oil in a large frying pan. Add the onions and fry over a high heat for 3–4 minutes. Cover the pan with a lid and cook the onions gently for about 20 minutes until soft. Remove the lid and continue to fry for a minute to evaporate the liquid. Add the sugar and vinegar and fry for another couple of minutes until golden. Remove the onions from the pan and set them aside to cool.

3   Add the remaining oil to the pan and place over a high heat. Add the mushrooms and fry for 2–3 minutes. Cover the pan with a lid and cook for 3–4 minutes, then remove the lid and fry over a high heat to evaporate the liquid. Remove the mushrooms with a slotted spoon and add them to the onions.

4   Unroll the pastry on to the lined baking sheet and cut off a 2cm (¾in) strip around the edge. Brush over a border of 2cm (¾in) around the large sheet of pastry with some beaten egg. Sit the pastry strips on top, pressing them down lightly to make a raised border. Prick the base inside the border with a fork and brush the border with a little more beaten egg.

5   Whisk the cream into the remaining egg in a bowl. Pour in the cream, add the herbs and season. Stir in the grated cheese.

6   Spoon the onions and mushrooms on to the pastry, keeping them inside the border. Scatter the artichokes over the top. Season well and spoon the egg mixture on top of the vegetables. Bake in the oven for 25–30 minutes until the pastry is crisp and golden brown. Serve hot, with a dressed tomato salad.

Paneer & roasted vegetable curry

Paneer is a fresh Indian cheese that does not have a strong flavour but stays firm when roasted. It combines beautifully with the vegetables in this delicious curry. Lovely served with some cooked rice.

SERVES 4–6

4 tbsp sunflower oil

1 cauliflower, broken into florets

300g sweet potato, cut into 2cm (¾in) dice

225g (8oz) paneer, cut into 2cm (¾in) dice

2 onions, sliced

3cm (1¼in) knob of fresh root ginger, peeled and grated

1 tbsp curry powder

1 tbsp garam masala

¼ tsp ground cloves

2 tbsp plain flour

600ml (1 pint) hot vegetable stock

2 tbsp mango chutney

150ml (5fl oz) double cream

100g (4oz) baby spinach

Juice of 1 lemon

Salt and freshly ground black pepper

1   Preheat the oven to 220°C/200°C fan/Gas 7.

2   Drizzle 2 tablespoons of the oil into a large roasting tin. Scatter the pieces of cauliflower and sweet potato into the tin and toss to coat them with oil. Season with salt and pepper.

3   Roast in the oven for about 15 minutes. Add the paneer at one end of the hot roasting tin and return it to the oven. Cook for 5–10 minutes, turning halfway through, until the cheese is golden on both sides, the cauliflower is golden and the sweet potato is tender. Set aside.

4   Heat the remaining oil in a large deep frying pan. Add the onions and ginger and fry for 5–10 minutes until cooked. Sprinkle in the spices and flour and stir over the heat for a few seconds. Gradually pour in the stock and stir until thickened, then simmer for a few minutes over a high heat.

5   Stir in the mango chutney and cream, then add the roasted cauliflower and sweet potato to the pan. Stir in the spinach until it has heated through and wilted, then add the lemon juice and check the seasoning.

6   Add the paneer at the last moment and serve piping hot.

Mixed bean & butternut wraps

I am really into wraps – they're quick to make and easy to eat.
Perfect for lunch on the go. To make your own wraps, see page 59.

MAKES 4

400g (14oz) peeled butternut
squash, cut into 3cm (1½in)
dice
1 tbsp olive oil
2 tsp ground cumin
200g (7oz) soured cream
4 spring onions, thinly sliced
½ small garlic clove, crushed
1 tbsp harissa paste
Juice of ½ lemon
1 x 400g (14oz) tin of mixed
beans, rinsed and drained
Small bunch of coriander,
chopped
1 small romaine lettuce, finely
sliced
4 wraps
Salt and freshly ground black
pepper

1   Preheat the oven to 220°C/200°C/ fan/Gas 7.

2   Put the squash on a baking sheet, drizzle it with oil, then season
with a teaspoon of the cumin and sprinkle with salt and pepper.
Roast the squash for about 15 minutes until lightly golden, then
leave to cool.

3   Measure the soured cream into a small bowl, add the remaining
ground cumin, the spring onions, garlic, harissa paste and lemon
juice and mix together. Stir in the beans and chopped coriander
and season well.

4   Warm the wraps in the cooling oven until just warm to the touch
but not brittle.

5   Put some lettuce in the middle of each wrap and top with the
bean mixture and squash. Fold in the sides and bottom, then
roll up tightly and slice in half on the diagonal.

Posh jacket potatoes

Here are lots of lovely filling ideas to dress up plain jacket potatoes. They are great for feeding a crowd and the ultimate comfort food. Each topping is enough for 4 potatoes – 8 halves.

SERVES 4–8

4 large baking potatoes,
    scrubbed clean
2 tbsp milk
A knob of butter
Olive oil, for drizzling
Salt and freshly ground black
    pepper
Chopped parsley, to garnish

FOR THE TOPPINGS

RED PEPPER & GOAT'S CHEESE

2 large red peppers, halved and
    deseeded
Olive oil, for drizzling
1 tbsp soft goat's cheese
1 tbsp chopped basil leaves

PESTO

3 tbsp basil pesto
75g (3oz) Parmesan cheese,
    coarsely grated
2 tbsp chopped parsley

SPRING ONION & SOURED CREAM

4 spring onions, chopped
Dash of vegetable oil
4 heaped tbsp soured cream
Paprika, for dusting

BACON & MUSHROOM

4 rashers of bacon
50g (2oz) button mushrooms,
    sliced
50g (2oz) mature Cheddar
    cheese, grated

1 Preheat the oven to 220°C/200°C fan/Gas 7 and bake the potatoes for about an hour or until soft in the middle.

2 Slice each potato in half and scoop out the soft potato into a bowl. Add the milk and butter and mash with a fork. Stir in the topping of your choice (see below), season and mix to combine.

3 Spoon the mixture back into the skins and sit the potatoes, filled side up, in a roasting tin. Drizzle over a little olive oil and return to the oven for about 15 minutes or until golden and the skins are crisp. Sprinkle with parsley and serve hot.

RED PEPPER & GOAT'S CHEESE Place the pepper halves on a baking sheet, skin side up, and drizzle them with a little olive oil. Roast in a preheated oven, 200°C/180°C fan/Gas 6, for about 15 minutes until blackened and soft, then peel off the skins and cut into thin strips. Alternatively, buy a jar of chargrilled peppers in a jar and slice 2 of them. Stir the pepper strips into the soft potato, season well and add the goat's cheese and basil leaves.

PESTO Simply add the filling ingredients to the soft potato, season and mix well.

SPRING ONION & SOURED CREAM Fry the spring onions in a little oil over a high heat until soft. Add them to the soft potato, season well, then stir in the soured cream. Dust the potatoes with a little paprika.

BACON & MUSHROOM Cut the bacon pieces into small pieces and fry until crisp, then add the mushrooms and fry over a high heat for a few minutes. Mix with the soft potato, season well and top with the grated cheese.

PREPARE AHEAD
Can fill the potatoes ready for their second bake up to 4 hours ahead. To reheat, cook at the same temperature as above, but for 30 minutes. Cover with foil if the tops are getting too brown.

Cauliflower, broccoli & leek Mornay

A truly comforting meal, this dish just needs a side of warm crusty bread.

SERVES 4-6

500g (1lb 2oz) cauliflower,
  cut into medium florets
350g (12oz) broccoli, cut into
  medium florets
2 small leeks, thickly sliced
Salt and freshly ground black
  pepper

FOR THE SAUCE

75g (3oz) butter
75g (3oz) plain flour
900ml (1½ pints) hot milk
1 tbsp Dijon mustard
75g (3oz) mature Cheddar
  cheese, grated
75g (3oz) Parmesan cheese,
  finely grated
Sprinkle of paprika

PREPARE AHEAD
*Can be assembled up to
12 hours ahead.*

1 You will need a large, shallow, ovenproof dish with a capacity of 1.8 litres (3¼ pints) and measuring about 25 x 15 x 5cm (10 x 6 x 2in). Preheat the oven to 180°C/160°C fan/Gas 4.

2 Bring a shallow pan of salted water to the boil. Add the cauliflower, bring to the boil and continue to boil for about 1½ minutes. Add the broccoli to the pan and boil for 1 minute. Remove the vegetables with a slotted spoon, reserving the cooking water. Drain the vegetables in a colander and then refresh under cold water until cold. Drain well and set aside.

3 Add the leeks to the cooking water and boil for about 7 minutes until just tender. Drain them in a colander and refresh under cold water until cold. Drain well and set aside.

4 Arrange the vegetables in the dish, making sure they are evenly mixed so each spoonful will have all three vegetables in a scoop! Season with salt and pepper.

5 For the sauce, melt the butter in the pan, sprinkle in the flour and stir over the heat for a few seconds. Add the hot milk and whisk until the sauce is smooth and thickened. Add the mustard, seasoning and three-quarters of the cheeses.

6 Spoon the sauce into the dish, coating the vegetables. Sprinkle with the remaining cheese and paprika. Bake in the oven for about 20-25 minutes until piping hot and golden on top. Be careful not to overcook or the vegetables will give off liquid. Leave to stand for a few minutes before serving.

Leek & dill quiche with a choice of toppings

A new and easy way to serve quiche – make a delicious simple base, then choose from a selection of toppings.

SERVES 6

FOR THE PASTRY

125g (4½ oz) plain flour, plus extra for dusting
75g (3oz) butter, cubed
25g (1oz) Parmesan cheese, grated
1 egg yolk, beaten with 1 tbsp water

FOR THE FILLING

25g (1oz) butter
3 small leeks, finely sliced
1 bunch of dill, chopped
4 large eggs
300ml (10fl oz) pouring double cream
100g (4oz) mature Cheddar cheese, grated
Salt and freshly ground black pepper

TOPPING IDEAS

6 slices of smoked salmon
Parma ham and avocado
Crispy bacon
Cherry tomatoes and fresh basil
Prawns and avocado
Sautéed garlic mushrooms
Blanched asparagus tips and rock salt

PREPARE AHEAD
Can be made up to a day ahead. Reheat to serve, then add the topping.

FREEZE
Freezes well once cooked.

1 You will need a 20cm (8in) round, loose-bottomed, fluted tart tin. Preheat the oven to 200°c/180°c fan/Gas 6.

2 To make the pastry, measure the flour, butter and cheese into a food processor and whizz until the mixture resembles breadcrumbs. Add the beaten egg yolk and water and whizz to a ball of dough. Alternatively, rub the flour, butter and cheese together in a mixing bowl with your fingertips before adding the egg yolk and water.

3 Roll the pastry out on a lightly floured work surface to a disc slightly larger than the tin. Carefully transfer the pastry to the tin and press it into the base and sides. Form a lip of pastry around the edges of the tin. Prick the base with a fork and place in the fridge to chill for 30 minutes.

4 Line the pastry case with baking paper and baking beans, slide into the oven and bake blind for about 15 minutes. Remove the paper and beans and bake for another 5 minutes or until just cooked and pale golden. Reduce the oven temperature to 190°c/170°c fan/Gas 5.

5 Meanwhile, to make the filling, melt the butter in a saucepan. Add the leeks and fry over a high heat, then cover the pan, lower the heat and cook for 10–15 minutes until soft. Leave the leeks to cool for 10 minutes, then spread them over the base of the tart. Sprinkle the dill over the leeks. Mix the eggs, cream and cheese together in a bowl, season with salt and pepper and pour into the pastry case.

6 Bake in the oven for about 30–35 minutes until just set in the middle. Leave to cool slightly, then slice into 6 wedges and arrange your chosen topping on each wedge.

Super veg with brown rice & herbs

This is such a great dish to have as a regular part of your weekday meals. Luc cooks it often and it can be served on its own in a bowl or with a grilled chicken breast. It's also good served cold as a rice salad.

SERVES 4–6

200g (7oz) brown long-grain rice
1 tbsp sunflower oil
50g (2oz) butter
1 onion, chopped
1 fennel bulb, core removed, thinly sliced
175g (6oz) butternut squash, peeled and diced into small cubes
1 garlic clove, crushed
150ml (5fl oz) white wine
2 small courgettes, diced
200g (7oz) chestnut mushrooms, sliced
Squeeze of lemon juice
3 tbsp chopped parsley
1 tbsp chopped thyme
2 tbsp toasted pumpkin seeds
Salt and freshly ground black pepper

PREPARE AHEAD
Can be made up to 8 hours ahead and served cold.

1 Cook the rice in boiling water according to the packet instructions. Drain and set aside.

2 Heat the oil and butter in a large frying pan. Add the onion, fennel and squash, then fry over high heat for 5 minutes. Add the garlic and fry for 10 seconds. Pour in the wine, cover the pan and simmer for 5 minutes until the squash is tender. Add the courgettes and mushrooms and fry for a few more minutes.

3 Toss in the cooked rice and lemon juice and stir over the heat until the rice is heated through. Add the herbs and season with salt and pepper. Serve sprinkled with pumpkin seeds.

Salads & Sides

Squash & parsnip roasties

Cooked together, these wonderful vegetables are a great accompaniment to any roast.

SERVES 4–6

3 tbsp sunflower oil

600g (1lb 5oz) large parsnips, peeled and cut into large 3cm (1½in) cubes

750g (1lb 10oz) butternut squash, peeled and cut into large 3cm (1½in) cubes

Sea salt

PREPARE AHEAD
Can be peeled and cubed, then kept covered in cold water for up to 4 hours. Drain and dry before roasting.

1　Preheat the oven to 220°c/200°c fan/Gas 7. Slide a large roasting tin into the oven to heat up.

2　Add the oil to the hot tin, tip in the parsnips and turn them once to coat in the oil.

3　Roast the parsnips for about 10 minutes, then remove the tin from the oven, add the squash and stir to coat it all in the oil. Continue to roast for about 30 minutes, turning once, until cooked through and golden brown. Sprinkle the roasties with sea salt before serving.

Fragrant lemongrass & coriander rice

Full of flavour, this rice is perfect with any curry. Bash the lemongrass stalk with
a rolling pin or the edge of a chopping board to break the edges of the fibres,
allowing the flavour to be released during cooking. Discard the lemongrass
at the end, as it will not be edible.

SERVES 4–6

1 tbsp sunflower oil
1 onion, finely chopped
1 garlic clove, crushed
½ fresh red chilli, deseeded
   and finely diced
225g (8oz) basmati rice
1 lemongrass stalk, bashed
Juice of 1 lime
Bunch of coriander, chopped
Salt and freshly ground black
   pepper
Coriander leaves, to serve
Lime wedges, to serve

PREPARE AHEAD
*Can be made up to an hour ahead
and covered with foil to keep warm.*

1 Heat the oil in a wide-based saucepan. Add the onion, garlic and
   chilli and fry for a few minutes. Wash the rice in a sieve and add
   it to the pan, then stir to coat the grains. Add 500ml (18fl oz) of
   water and the lemongrass.

2 Cover the pan with a lid and bring to the boil. Simmer for about
   15 minutes over a low heat until all the water has been absorbed
   and the grains of rice are separate.

3 Remove the lemongrass, then add the lime juice and coriander.
   Season with salt and pepper and stir gently. Spoon into a bowl
   and serve garnished with coriander and lime wedges.

Ridged garlic potatoes

A different but classic French way to serve potatoes. They are half-poached, half-roasted and are tender and full of flavour.

SERVES 4

75g (3oz) butter, softened
1kg (2lb 3oz) medium-sized
   potatoes, such as Maris Piper,
   sliced into 1cm (½in) slices
150ml (5fl oz) chicken stock
1 garlic clove, crushed
Salt and freshly ground black
   pepper

PREPARE AHEAD
*Can be part-baked in the stock
6 hours ahead, then roasted before
serving.*

1   You will need a shallow 1.75-litre (3-pint) roasting tin or ovenproof dish. Preheat the oven to 200°C/180°C fan/Gas 6.

2   Use 25g (1oz) of the butter to grease the tin. Fan out the sliced potatoes in neat overlapping rows and season well with salt and pepper. Pour over the stock and bake in the oven for about 30 minutes. Mix the remaining butter with the crushed garlic.

3   Remove the tin from the oven and dot the garlic butter over the potatoes. Turn up the heat to 220°C/200°C fan/Gas 7 and bake for a further 15 minutes until the potatoes are golden and crisp on top.

Colcannon mash

A traditional Irish side dish, this is a hearty filler, using inexpensive ingredients.
Originally it was made with just mashed potato and cabbage or kale, but adding milk
and cream updates it and makes a richer version.

SERVES 6

450g (1lb) potatoes, cubed
2 tbsp milk
2 tbsp double cream
A couple of knobs of butter
½ small pointed cabbage,
    shredded
4 spring onions, thinly sliced
Salt and freshly ground black
    pepper

PREPARE AHEAD
*Can be made up to 3 hours ahead
and gently reheated in a dish in a
low oven.*

1 Place the potatoes in a pan of cold salted water. Cover with
   a lid, bring to the boil and cook for about 15 minutes or until
   tender. Drain in a colander.

2 Put the milk, cream and a knob of butter into the pan and heat,
   then add the drained potatoes. Mash until smooth and season
   with salt and pepper.

3 Heat the remaining butter in a frying pan. Add the cabbage
   and spring onions and fry over a medium heat for 5-6 minutes
   until tender.

4 Add the cabbage and onions to the mashed potatoes and mix
   well, then lightly beat together using a fork. Serve in a warm bowl.

The best roast potatoes

A roast potato should be ultra-crispy and golden on the outside with a fluffy light middle. Par-boiling the potatoes ahead and roughing them up before roasting gives a lovely crispy outside, with the semolina adding extra crunch. If you don't have any goose fat, use extra sunflower oil.

SERVES 6

1kg (2lb 3oz) potatoes, such as Maris Piper or King Edward, cut into medium-sized chunks
50g (2oz) semolina
3 tbsp goose fat
3 tbsp sunflower oil
Salt

PREPARE AHEAD
Can be roasted up to 12 hours ahead. Before serving, reheat in a hot oven for 15–20 minutes – no need to add extra fat.

1 Preheat the oven to 220°C/200°C fan/Gas 7.

2 Put the potato chunks in a pan of cold salted water. Bring to the boil and boil for about 5 minutes until the potatoes are starting to soften around the edges. Drain in a colander until completely dry, tip back into the pan and shake to rough up the edges. Sprinkle in the semolina and shake again until coated.

3 Preheat a roasting tin in the oven until hot. Add the goose fat and oil and heat for 5 minutes until smoking. Add the potatoes and turn them in the fat until coated. Return to the oven and roast for about 45–55 minutes until the potatoes are golden brown and crisp, turning them over halfway through the cooking time. Serve piping hot.

Yorkshire pudding

I guarantee success if you follow this recipe for Yorkshire pudding, which I have been making to serve with Sunday lunches for many years.

SERVES 6–8

100g (4oz) plain flour
¼ tsp salt
3 large eggs
225ml (8fl oz) milk
Sunflower oil

PREPARE AHEAD
Can be made and cooked ahead and then reheated in a hot oven, 220°C/200°C fan/Gas 7, for about 8 minutes. The batter can be made up to 12 hours ahead.

FREEZE
These freeze well.

1 You will need a 12-hole deep bun tin, or two 4-hole Yorkshire pudding tins or a large 23 x 33cm (9 x 13in) roasting tin. Preheat the oven to 220°C/200°C fan/Gas 7.

2 Measure the flour and salt into a bowl and make a well in the centre. Add the eggs and a little of the milk. Whisk until smooth, then gradually add the remaining milk and mix to combine. You can use a wooden spoon but it's easier with an electric hand whisk. Pour the mixture into a jug.

3 Measure a dessertspoon of oil into each hole of the 12-bun tray, or a tablespoon into each hole of the 4-hole tins, or 3 tablespoons into the roasting tin. Transfer to the preheated oven for about 5 minutes or until the oil is piping hot.

4 Carefully remove the tin from the oven and pour the batter equally between the holes or into the roasting tin. Quickly return the batter to the oven and cook for about 20–25 minutes or until golden brown and well risen. Serve immediately.

Potato wedges with soured cream chive dip

These potato wedges are a firm family favourite the world over and as they're made in the oven, they are healthier than the deep-fried versions.

SERVES 4–6

600g (1lb 5oz) medium
  potatoes, skins on
2 tbsp olive oil
2 tbsp semolina
Salt and freshly ground black
  pepper

FOR THE DIP
150ml (5fl oz) soured cream
2 tbsp chopped chives
½ small garlic clove, crushed

PREPARE AHEAD
Dip can be made up to
2 days ahead.

1 Line a large baking sheet with non-stick baking paper. Preheat the oven to 220°C/200°C fan/Gas 7.

2 Cut the potatoes in half and slice each half into fat wedges. Place them in a bowl, add the oil and semolina, then season with salt and pepper. Toss until all the wedges are coated and arrange on the lined baking sheet.

3 Bake in the oven for about 30 minutes or until the potatoes are golden and cooked through.

4 Measure the dip ingredients into a bowl, season well with salt and pepper and mix to combine. Spoon the dip into a bowl and serve alongside the hot potato wedges.

Split roasted butternut squash with chilli garlic butter

I love all squash, but I particularly enjoy the nutty flavour of the butternut and its lovely vibrant colour.

SERVES 4–6

1 butternut squash
1–2 tbsp olive oil, for drizzling
50g (2oz) butter, softened
1 tbsp chopped parsley
1 tbsp chopped chives
1 small garlic clove, crushed
½ fresh red chilli, deseeded and finely diced
Salt and freshly ground black pepper

PREPARE AHEAD
Chilli garlic butter can be made up to a week ahead.

FREEZE
Butter freezes well.

1 Preheat the oven to 220°C/200°C fan/Gas 7.

2 Slice the squash in half lengthways and scoop out the seeds. Sit the halves, cut side up, in a roasting tin. Season well and drizzle with olive oil.

3 Pour 300ml (10fl oz) of water into the base of the tin around the squash. Roast for about 45–60 minutes, depending on the size of the squash, or until the flesh is soft.

4 While the squash is roasting, mash the butter with the herbs, garlic and chilli. Place the butter on a piece of cling film and roll the cling film around the butter to make a cylinder. Seal the ends and chill in the fridge for 30 minutes.

5 When the squash is cooked and golden, slice the butter into rounds and place on top of the squash to melt gently. Serve the squash on wooden boards with spoons for scooping out.

Carrot & swede purée

This purée has a lovely vibrant colour and is full of flavour. It's great to use home-grown root vegetables if you can, and these are at their best in the autumn and winter months.

SERVES 4–6

675g (1½lb) carrots, sliced
675g (1½lb) swede, chopped
  into small cubes
A knob of butter
¼ tsp nutmeg
Salt and freshly ground black
  pepper

PREPARE AHEAD
*Can be made up to 4 hours
ahead and reheated, covered
with foil, in a dish.*

1 Put the vegetables into a pan and cover with salted water. Bring to the boil and simmer for about 20 minutes until completely soft. Drain well.

2 Add the butter and nutmeg and, using a hand blender, blend to a smooth purée. Season with salt and pepper to taste.

Sweet potato skinny fries

Quick to make, these are healthier than regular fries but the children will still be delighted! You can use the same method with white potatoes, but leave the skins on so they hold their shape, and cook them for a little longer than the sweet potato version.

SERVES 4–6

3 large sweet potatoes
1 tbsp olive oil
Sea salt

1 Preheat the oven to 220°C/200°C fan/Gas 7.

2 Peel the sweet potatoes and cut them into thin fries. Tip them on to a baking sheet, drizzle with the oil and toss well. Make sure they are in a single layer in the tin and not overlapping.

3 Bake the fries for 20 minutes, then turn them over and return to the oven for a further 15–20 minutes or until tender. Sprinkle with sea salt, toss and serve straight away.

Pickled beetroot

One of my favourite vegetables to grow and eat, beetroot reminds me of weekends at home – those family days when the table was laden with hams, cheeses and pickles and beetroot was always there. Beetroot is expensive to buy ready cooked but it's simple, and much cheaper, to prepare it yourself. A useful tip – don't cut the stalks off completely or the colour will bleed out of the beetroot when cooking. If there's any sweetened vinegar left in the container once the beetroot is finished, boil it up and use it in the next batch.

MAKES 2 X 450G (1LB) JARS

750g (1lb 10oz) small raw
   beetroot
50g (2oz) caster sugar
About 75ml (3fl oz) white wine
   vinegar
Salt and freshly ground black
   pepper

1 You will need a lidded reusable glass container. Do not use a metal container – the pickling liquid will react with the metal and tarnish the beetroot.

2 Trim the stalks of the beetroot but leave about 2.5cm (1in) attached. (You can use the rest of the stalks in a salad. Just cut into batons and boil for 3 minutes, then mix with other salad leaves and dress.)

3 Place the beetroot in a saucepan and cover with cold water. Bring to the boil and boil for 50–60 minutes until soft to the point of a knife. Drain and leave to cool, then peel off the skin. Slice the beetroot into rounds.

4 Put a layer of beetroot slices in the container and sprinkle over some sugar and seasoning. Continue to layer until you have used up all the sugar and beetroot, then pour over the vinegar just to cover.

5 Put the lid on and gently turn the container to mix. Leave for 30 minutes before serving. This keeps for 3 weeks in the fridge.

Golden roasted vegetables

Instead of just serving roast potatoes with a Sunday meal, try this wonderful
variety of colours and textures. Do not overcook the beetroot, or the colour
will bleed into the other vegetables.

SERVES 4-6

4 tbsp sunflower oil

500g (1lb 2oz) butternut squash,
   peeled and cut into 4cm
   (1¾in) cubes

350g (12oz) sweet potato, peeled
   and cut into 4cm (1¾in) cubes

250g (9oz) beetroot, peeled and
   cut into 4cm (1¾in) cubes

250g (9oz) parsnips, peeled and
   cut into 4cm (1¾in) cubes

500g (1lb 2oz) cauliflower,
   broken into large florets

Salt and freshly ground black
   pepper

PREPARE AHEAD

*Cook the vegetables until golden,
then leave to cool in the tins. Reheat
in a preheated oven, 220°C/ 200°C
fan/Gas 7, for 15 minutes until
heated through.*

1 You will need two large roasting tins. Preheat the oven to 220°C/
   200°C fan/Gas 7.

2 Divide the oil between the roasting tins, then slide the tins into
   the oven for 5 minutes to heat up.

3 Put the squash, sweet potato and beetroot into one tin and toss
   together in the oil. Season well. Put the parsnip and cauliflower
   into the other tin, then toss in the oil and season.

4 Put both tins into the oven and roast for 30–40 minutes until the
   vegetables are golden and cooked through. The cauliflower and
   parsnips will take less time and be ready after 30 minutes. Keep
   an eye on the vegetables and turn them about three times so they
   cook evenly.

Simmered red cabbage & cider

Red cabbage is a hearty vegetable and perfect to serve in the autumn
as a delicious accompaniment to game dishes.

SERVES 6

1 tbsp olive oil
2 knobs of butter
1 onion, sliced
1kg (2lb 3oz) red cabbage,
   finely shredded
250ml (10fl oz) cider
4 tbsp redcurrant jelly
Salt and freshly ground black
   pepper

PREPARE AHEAD
*Can be made up to 12 hours ahead.
To reheat, put into an ovenproof
dish, cover with foil and bake in
a moderate oven until hot, or stir
gently in a pan on the hob.*

FREEZE
Freezes well once cooked.

1 Preheat the oven to 160°C/140°C fan/Gas 3.

2 Heat the oil and a knob of the butter in a deep ovenproof
   saucepan. Add the onion and cabbage and fry for 3–4 minutes.
   Add the cider and redcurrant jelly, season with salt and pepper,
   bring to the boil and boil for a few minutes.

3 Cover the pan with a lid and place in the oven for 3–4 hours until
   completely tender. Using a slotted spoon, transfer the cabbage to
   a warm dish, leaving the juices behind in the pan.

4 Place the pan on the hob and reduce the liquid until the colour
   has darkened and it has reduced to a syrupy consistency. Stir in
   the remaining butter, remove the pan from the heat and pour the
   syrupy liquid over the cabbage in the dish.

Stir-fried aromatic Hispi cabbage

A lovely green vegetable side, this is great served with Asian dishes. Pointed cabbage, known also as Hispi cabbage or sweetheart cabbage, is slightly softer than white cabbage but not as floppy as Savoy cabbage, so it's perfect for a stir-fry.

SERVES 4

1 tbsp olive oil
A knob of butter
2 banana shallots, coarsely sliced
1 Hispi cabbage, core removed, finely shredded
½ tbsp ground cumin
Salt and freshly ground black pepper

1 Heat the oil and butter in a large frying pan. Add the shallots and fry them over a high heat for about 3 minutes until starting to soften but not browned.

2 Add the cabbage and quickly stir-fry until the leaves have just wilted but still have crunch. Season with salt and pepper and sprinkle with cumin. Fry for another minute and serve in a warm bowl.

Greek salad with feta & olive tapenade

A beautiful salad, this has the classic flavours of feta cheese, mint, cucumber and tomato. Instead of olives, we have used quenelles of olive tapenade and feta to make the dish a little more luxurious.

SERVES 4

350g (12oz) mixed heritage
   tomatoes
½ cucumber
6 spring onions, sliced
Small bunch of mint, chopped
100g (4oz) soft feta cheese
1 tbsp mayonnaise
3–4 tbsp black olive tapenade
Salt and freshly ground black
   pepper

FOR THE DRESSING

6 tbsp olive oil
2 tbsp red wine vinegar
1 tsp sugar

PREPARE AHEAD
*The salad can be made an hour
ahead and dressed before serving.
Quenelles can be made up to
3 hours ahead and kept in the fridge.*

1   Mix all the dressing ingredients in a bowl.

2   Slice and quarter the tomatoes and put them in a mixing bowl. Slice the cucumber in half lengthways, then slice thinly on the diagonal and add to the bowl. Scatter over the spring onions and mint and season with salt and pepper. Add the dressing and toss lightly to combine.

3   Using a fork, mash the feta in a small bowl. Add the mayonnaise and mix well.

4   Divide the salad between pretty bowls or plates. Using a couple of spoons, shape the feta mixture into 4 oval quenelles and sit one on top of each serving of salad. Shape the olive tapenade into quenelles in the same way and place one next to each feta quenelle. Serve with crunchy bread.

Roasted pepper & tomato salad with broad beans

A vibrant, tasty salad, this is slightly different from the usual pepper salad and full of flavour. Removing the greyish outer skins from the beans is a bit time-consuming but we think it makes all the difference to the salad. If time is short, though, leave the beans in their skins.

SERVES 6

3 red peppers, halved and deseeded
250g (9oz) frozen broad beans
200g (7oz) rocket leaves
400g (14oz) cherry tomatoes, halved

FOR THE BASIL & GARLIC DRESSING
3 tbsp olive oil
1 tbsp balsamic vinegar
1 tbsp chopped basil
½ garlic clove, crushed

PREPARE AHEAD
Can be assembled up to 2 hours ahead. Dress just before serving.

1 Line a baking sheet with baking paper. Preheat the oven to 220°C/200°C fan/Gas 7.

2 Put the peppers, cut side down, on the baking sheet and roast for about 25–30 minutes until the skins are blackened. Place the peppers in a bowl, cover with cling film and leave to cool. Once cool, peel the skins off and slice the peppers into thick slices.

3 Cook the broad beans in boiling, salted water for 3–4 minutes, or until tender. Drain and run under cold water, then remove the grey outer skins to reveal the bright green beans.

4 To make the dressing, mix all the ingredients together in a small jug.

5 Scatter the rocket over a serving dish and top with the peppers, broad beans and tomatoes. Just before serving, season with pepper and rock salt and pour over the dressing.

Rosy-pink beetroot, feta & olive salad

The sharpness of the olives and beetroot contrasts so well with the rich creaminess of the feta. The red onion dressing is a pretty pink like the radishes and gives great texture to the salad. Choose pitted or whole olives as you prefer – most of the most flavoursome olives have stones in them.

SERVES 6–8

100g (4oz) ciabatta bread
1 tbsp olive oil
50g (2oz) rocket leaves
2 Little Gem lettuces, sliced
  lengthways into strips
150g (5oz) black olives
600g (1lb 5oz) cooked beetroot,
  diced into 2cm cubes
200g (7oz) radishes, thinly
  sliced into discs
200g (7oz) feta cheese,
  crumbled into large pieces
Salt and freshly ground black
  pepper

FOR THE BALSAMIC
RED ONION DRESSING
2 tbsp balsamic vinegar
6 tbsp olive oil
1 tsp caster sugar
1 red onion, finely sliced

PREPARE AHEAD
*Croutons can be made up to a
week ahead. Assemble the salad
up to 4 hours ahead and dress
before serving.*

1 Preheat the oven to 200°C/180°C fan/Gas 6.

2 Slice the bread into 1cm (½in) cubes. Toss them in the oil and then spread out on a baking sheet. Bake in the oven for about 12 minutes until crispy and lightly golden, turning them once. Transfer the croutons to a plate lined with kitchen paper, sprinkle with salt and pepper, then leave to cool.

3 To make the dressing, measure the vinegar, oil and sugar into a bowl. Season with a little salt and pepper and whisk until smooth. Add the red onion, mix to combine and leave to marinate for about 30 minutes.

4 Put the rocket leaves and lettuce strips into a salad bowl. Scatter over the olives, beetroot, radishes, feta and croutons Season with salt and pepper and pour over the dressing just before serving.

Roasted pepper, mushroom & broccoli brown rice salad

This recipe is Lucy's favourite weekday dish. It's so versatile – you can add cooked chicken, prawns or bacon if you like. It's good served cold or warm.

SERVES 4–6

175g (6oz) brown rice
2 red onions, fairly thinly sliced
2 Romano peppers, halved and
    deseeded
1 tbsp olive oil
200g (7oz) button mushrooms,
    thinly sliced
150g (5oz) tenderstem broccoli,
    halved lengthways and stems
    cut into slices
4 tbsp chopped parsley
2 tbsp chopped basil
Salt and freshly ground black
    pepper

FOR THE DRESSING
3 tbsp olive oil
1 small garlic clove, crushed
Zest and juice of 1 small lemon
1 tbsp sweet chilli sauce

PREPARE AHEAD
*Can be assembled up to 4 hours
ahead, then dressed up to an hour
before serving.*

1 You will need a baking sheet lined with non-stick baking paper. Preheat the oven to 220°c/200°c fan/Gas 7.

2 Cook the rice in boiling salted water according to the packet instructions, then drain and leave to cool.

3 Put the onions and peppers on the baking sheet and drizzle with the oil. Sprinkle with salt and pepper, toss, then spread the vegetables out in an even layer. Roast for 15 minutes, scatter in the mushrooms and return to the oven for 5 minutes. Remove from the oven and peel off the skin from the peppers. Cut the peppers into thick slices and put them in a bowl with the onions.

4 Bring a pan of water to the boil, add the broccoli and blanch for 2–3 minutes. Drain and run under cold water until cool, then drain again well.

5 Add the broccoli, mushrooms and rice to the bowl of onions and peppers. Add the herbs, season and mix well.

6 Measure the dressing ingredients into a jug and whisk until combined. Pour over the salad and toss well.

Puddings

Celebration trifle

This is the trifle I make year after year and all the family love it. Be sure to whisk
the egg mixture quickly when pouring in the cream and milk. This cools the mixture
and makes a smooth custard base. It's also important to let the custard
thicken gently over simmering heat.

SERVES 6

FOR THE TRIFLE CUSTARD
50g (2oz) caster sugar
3 tbsp cornflour
4 egg yolks
1 tbsp vanilla extract
450ml (15fl oz) full-fat milk
150ml (5fl oz) double cream

FOR THE TRIFLE
6 trifle sponges
½ jar of raspberry jam
1 x 400g (14oz) tin of pears,
   pears sliced and juice reserved
4 tbsp sherry
250g (9oz) raspberries
150ml (5fl oz) double cream,
   lightly whipped
25g (1oz) flaked almonds,
   lightly toasted

PREPARE AHEAD
Can be made up to 8 hours ahead.

1 You will need a shallow trifle dish with a capacity of about
   1.5 litres (2½ pints).

2 For the custard, measure the caster sugar, cornflour, egg yolks
   and vanilla extract into a mixing bowl and whisk together.
   Warm the milk and cream in a saucepan until just simmering.

3 Pour the hot milk and cream into the egg mixture and whisk
   quickly until smooth. Rinse out the saucepan, then pour the
   mixture through a sieve into the clean pan. Heat over a medium
   heat, whisking all the time until the custard has thickened.
   Be careful not to let it boil. Remove the pan from the heat and
   pour the custard into a bowl. Cover with cling film and leave the
   custard to cool, then place it in the fridge to chill.

4 Slice the trifle sponges in half, spread them with jam and
   sandwich together. Arrange them over the base of the dish.
   You might need to trim the sponges to make them fit.

5 Spoon over 6 tablespoons of the pear juice and the sherry. Press
   the sponges down with the back of a spoon to encourage them
   to absorb all the liquid – add a little more pear juice if necessary.
   Scatter the sliced pears and half the raspberries over the sponges,
   then pour over the cold custard. Put the trifle in the fridge to set
   for a few hours or overnight.

6 When you're ready to serve, spoon blobs of cream on top of the
   custard, decorate with the rest of the raspberries and sprinkle
   with toasted almonds.

Lemon posset tart with fresh raspberries

Simple to make, this delicious lemon tart is set in the fridge, not baked. It is quite deep, so it's best made in a loose-bottomed sandwich tin, as for a Victoria sponge.

SERVES 8

FOR THE SHORTCRUST
PASTRY
175g (6oz) plain flour, plus extra
   for dusting
75g (3oz) cold butter, cubed
1 tbsp icing sugar
1 egg, beaten

FOR THE LEMON FILLING
600ml (1 pint) double cream
150g (5oz) caster sugar
Finely grated zest and juice
   of 3 lemons

TO SERVE
250g (9oz) raspberries
Icing sugar, for dusting

PREPARE AHEAD
Tart can be made up to a day ahead.
Decorate on the day.

1   You will need a 20cm (8in) round, deep, loose-bottomed sandwich tin. Preheat the oven to 200°C/180°C fan/Gas 6.

2   First make the pastry. Measure the flour, butter and icing sugar into a food processor and whizz until the mixture resembles breadcrumbs. Add the egg and whizz until the mixture comes together. Alternatively, rub the flour, butter and sugar together in a mixing bowl with your fingertips before adding the egg.

3   Remove the dough from the bowl and gather together on a floured work surface, then lightly knead until smooth (be careful not to over-knead). Roll the pastry out thinly and transfer it to the tin, lining the base and sides. Trim the edges and prick the base with a fork, then chill in the fridge for about 30 minutes.

4   Line the pastry case with baking paper and baking beans and bake blind in the oven for about 15 minutes. Remove the paper and beans and return to the oven for a further 5–7 minutes until completely cooked, crisp and pale golden. Set aside to cool.

5   To make the filling, pour the cream into a shallow saucepan. Add the sugar and lemon zest. Stir over the heat until just boiling and the sugar is dissolved, then remove the pan from the heat and leave to stand for 5 minutes. Stir in the lemon juice and stir until the consistency has thickened slightly. Leave to cool for 5 minutes, then spoon the filling into the tart case and level the top. Place in the fridge to chill for at least 4 hours or overnight.

6   Decorate with raspberries and dust with icing sugar. Serve sliced into wedges with some pouring cream if you like.

Divine white chocolate chilled cheesecake

Chocolate and cheesecake are both so popular and this combination is to die for! The cream cheese must be full fat. If you use a lighter version the cheesecake may not set.

SERVES 6–8

FOR THE BASE
50g (2oz) butter
150g (5oz) digestive biscuits, crushed

FOR THE FILLING
300g (11oz) good white chocolate, broken into pieces
2 x 180g (6oz) packs of full-fat cream cheese
200ml (7fl oz) pouring double cream

FOR DECORATION
50g (2oz) white chocolate, shaved into long curls

PREPARE AHEAD
Can be made up to a day ahead.

FREEZE
Freezes well.

1 You will need a 20cm (8in) round, deep, loose-bottomed sandwich tin. Line the base with a disc of non-stick baking paper. Remove the cream cheese from the fridge 15 minutes before using.

2 To make the base, melt the butter in a saucepan over a low heat. Add the crushed biscuits and stir them into the melted butter until coated. Spoon into the base of the prepared tin and use the back of the spoon to press down in an even layer. Chill in the fridge for 15 minutes.

3 Place the chocolate in a bowl set over a pan of gently simmering water, making sure the base of the bowl does not touch the water. Stir gently until the chocolate has just melted. Do not overheat or the chocolate may split and the cheesecake will not set.

4 Spoon the cream cheese and a quarter of the cream into a bowl. Gently whisk with an electric hand whisk until the mixture is smooth and there are no lumps. Pour in the rest of the cream and whisk again until smooth. Add the melted white chocolate and stir until fully incorporated into the cream mixture.

5 Spoon the mixture into the tin and level the surface. Chill in the fridge for at least 6 hours or ideally overnight.

6 Remove the cake from the tin, place on a serving plate and scatter over the white chocolate curls.

Wild bramble mousse

Pick your own blackberries in the late summer for this perfect light pudding – and freeze some to use later in the year as well. You can purée the blackberries in a food processor after cooking, as this makes it easier to pass them through a sieve.

SERVES 6

600g (1lb 5oz) blackberries
Juice of ½ lemon
175g (7oz) caster sugar
5 leaves of gelatine
150ml (5fl oz) pouring double cream
2 egg whites

TO SERVE

50g (2oz) blackberries
Icing sugar, for dusting
100ml (3½fl oz) whipped cream

PREPARE AHEAD
Can be made up to 2 days ahead.

1 You will need a 1.1-litre (2-pint) glass dish or 6 small dishes.

2 Tip the blackberries, lemon juice and 75g (3oz) of the caster sugar into a saucepan. Stir, cover the pan and simmer for 5–8 minutes until soft. Pass the blackberries through a sieve back into the pan, then discard the seeds. Reheat until piping hot.

3 Put the gelatine leaves into a bowl of cold water and leave for 5 minutes. Squeeze the water from the gelatine leaves and add them to the hot blackberry juice. Stir until dissolved. Set the mixture aside until it is cold and has thickened slightly.

4 Whip the cream to soft peaks. In a separate, clean bowl, whisk the egg whites, adding the remaining 100g (4oz) of caster sugar a teaspoon at a time. Keep whisking until all the sugar has been incorporated and the whites are stiff and look like a cloud (as for a meringue). Take care not to overwhisk or it will be tricky to incorporate the egg whites into the blackberries.

5 Add 2 large tablespoons of the whipped cream to the blackberry and gelatine mixture and stir in gently. Carefully fold in the rest of the cream and the egg whites until the mixture is smooth and light, with no white bits visible. Pour into the dish or dishes and place in the fridge for about 6 hours, or ideally overnight, to chill and set.

6 Decorate with a few blackberries, dust with icing sugar and serve with some whipped cream.

Lemon & blueberry mousse with hazelnut & oat topping

This very simple dessert combines the freshness of blueberries with zingy lemon mousse and a crunchy topping. It can be prepared ahead, so it's great for a party. Depending on the diameter of your serving glasses, you may have topping left over. Use it for breakfast or to sprinkle over yoghurt.

SERVES 6–8

FOR THE HAZELNUT
& OAT TOPPING

25g (1oz) butter

2 tbsp honey

100g (4oz) large porridge oats

50g (2oz) demerara sugar

50g (2oz) hazelnuts, roughly chopped

40g (1½oz) plain flour

FOR THE LEMON MOUSSE

200g (7oz) full-fat crème fraîche

200g (7oz) Greek yoghurt

3 tbsp luxury lemon curd

Juice of ½ lemon

200g (7oz) fresh blueberries

PREPARE AHEAD
Can be assembled up to 6 hours ahead and kept in the fridge. Topping can be made up to 3 days ahead.

1 You will need 6–8 small glasses and a baking sheet lined with baking paper. Preheat the oven to 180°C/160°C fan/Gas 4.

2 For the topping, melt the butter and honey in a saucepan. Add the other topping ingredients and spread the mixture out on the baking sheet. Bake for about 15–20 minutes, turning halfway through the cooking time, until golden brown. Remove from the oven and leave to cool on the tray until cold and crunchy.

3 To make the lemon mousse, mix the crème fraîche, yoghurt, lemon curd and lemon juice together in a bowl.

4 Divide the blueberries between the glasses and press them down firmly. Top with the lemon mixture and sprinkle with the topping.

Irish Cream and cherry pots

Chocolate and cherry go beautifully together, so I know these will be a firm favourite. They are fairly rich, so it's best to make them in small pots or glasses.

SERVES 8

180g (6oz) full-fat cream cheese, at room temperature

300ml (10fl oz) pouring double cream

2 tbsp icing sugar

6–8 tbsp Baileys Irish Cream

125g (5oz) sponge fingers (about 20 in total)

385g (13oz) jar of cherry compote

50g (2oz) Belgian white chocolate, chopped into small pieces

PREPARE AHEAD
Can be made up to a day ahead.
Serve at room temperature.

1 You will need 8 small pots or glasses.

2 Measure the cream cheese into a bowl. Gradually pour in the double cream and whisk until soft peaks form and the mixture is smooth but not too thick. Stir in the icing sugar.

3 Measure the Irish Cream into a shallow bowl. Add the sponge fingers and let them soak for a few minutes until starting to soften. Break half of them into smaller pieces and use them to line the base of the pots or glasses. Press down firmly.

4 Divide half the compote, then half the cream mixture between the pots. Repeat so you have two layers of each in each pot. Sprinkle the chopped chocolate on top, then leave to chill in the fridge for at least an hour.

Chocolate & raspberry layered pots

What is more comforting than chocolate? These little pots will make everyone smile
and they're so easy to make. They are very rich, so are made in small glasses.
Use Bournville chocolate, rather than one with a high cocoa solid percentage, as it is
less bitter. Cassis is a delicious blackcurrant liqueur, or you could use brandy instead.

MAKES 6–8

100g (4oz) Bournville dark
  chocolate
200ml (7fl oz) pouring double
  cream
150g (5oz) raspberries
1 tbsp icing sugar
1 tbsp cassis
100g (4oz) Belgian white
  chocolate

PREPARE AHEAD
Can be made up to 12 hours ahead.

1 You will need 6-8 little pots or glasses.

2 Break the plain chocolate into a small bowl. Heat half the cream
  in a saucepan until just boiling. Remove from the heat and pour
  the cream into the bowl of chocolate. Stir until melted, then set
  aside to cool for about 10 minutes.

3 Put 10 of the raspberries into a small bowl. Mash them with
  a fork and add the icing sugar and cassis. Add the remaining
  whole raspberries and stir to coat. Divide them between the
  pots or glasses.

4 Pour the dark chocolate mix on top of the raspberries and
  transfer the pots to the fridge until set (30-40 minutes).

5 Break the white chocolate into a small bowl. Heat the rest of
  the cream in a saucepan until just boiling. Remove from the heat
  and pour the cream into the bowl of white chocolate. Stir until
  melted, then set aside to cool for about 10 minutes.

6 Pour the white chocolate mix over the dark chocolate and put
  the pots back into the fridge for about an hour until set. Serve
  at room temperature.

Lemon ripple ice cream

Ice cream is always a comfort food, whether on its own in the summer to refresh you on a warm day or when served with a delicious dessert, such as the Toffee Pear Pudding on page 245, in winter. This recipe is so simple to make – no special ice cream machine needed.

SERVES 6

4 eggs, separated
100g (4oz) caster sugar
300ml (10fl oz) double cream
Finely grated zest of 2 lemons
305–325g (10½–11½oz) jar of
  luxury lemon curd

FREEZE
Freezes well for up to 3 months.

1 Put the egg whites into a large mixing bowl. Using an electric hand whisk, whisk on full speed until the whites look like a cloud. Gradually add the sugar, whisking on maximum speed, until you have a thick glossy meringue.

2 In a separate bowl, beat the egg yolks with a fork. Add them to the meringue mixture and stir until smooth.

3 Using an electric hand whisk, whisk the cream into soft peaks. Add the cream to the meringue with the lemon zest and half the curd. Gently fold together until smooth.

4 Spoon the mixture into a shallow container. Blob the remaining curd on top and swirl into the mixture to make a ripple effect. Freeze for at least 12 hours.

Decadent orange, chocolate & whisky mousse

Indulgent and delicious, this mousse has a classic combination of flavours.
It's the ultimate comfort food at any time of day!

SERVES 6–8

300ml (10fl oz) pouring double
   cream
150g (5oz) Bournville
   chocolate, broken into
   small pieces
1 large egg, separated
25g (1oz) caster sugar
1 tbsp whisky
Finely grated zest of ½ orange
Cocoa powder, to serve

PREPARE AHEAD
Can be made up to a day ahead.

1 You will need 6–8 ramekins or small pots.

2 Heat 150ml (5fl oz) of the double cream in a saucepan until
just hot. Remove from the heat and add the chocolate. Stir
until melted, then set aside to cool a little.

3 Pour the remaining cream into a bowl. Using an electric whisk,
whisk until soft peaks form. In a separate clean, dry bowl, whisk
the egg white until firm but not dry. Add the caster sugar, a
teaspoon at a time, and continue to whisk on a high speed until
glossy. Combine the meringue with the whipped cream.

4 Using a fork, mix the egg yolk with the whisky and orange zest in
a bowl. Add this to the chocolate mixture and stir until combined.
Then, using a metal spoon or flexible spatula, carefully fold this
into the whipped cream and meringue mixture, cutting and
folding until the mixture is smooth and light, with no white
showing. Don't beat the mixture, as you do not want to knock
the air out of the mousse.

5 Spoon into the pots and chill in the fridge for at least 4 hours
or overnight. Sprinkle with cocoa powder before serving.

Warming autumn fruit compote

This keeps well in the fridge and is a nice change from stodgy puddings on a cosy winter night. It's good for breakfast too.

SERVES 4

A small knob of butter

2 dessert apples, peeled, cored and thinly sliced

2 small star anise

50g (2oz) caster sugar

2 plums, stoned and sliced

150g (5oz) blueberries

150g (5oz) blackberries

200g (7oz) Greek yoghurt, to serve

PREPARE AHEAD
Can be made up to a day ahead and warmed gently to serve.

1 Melt the butter in a saucepan. Add the apples and star anise and cook them over the heat for a few minutes. Add the caster sugar and 150ml (5fl oz) of water, then stir for a few minutes to dissolve the sugar.

2 Bring to the boil and simmer the apples for 2 minutes. Add the plums and simmer for 2 minutes or until the fruits are nearly tender. Remove the pan from the heat, stir in the blueberries and blackberries and coat them in the syrup. Leave for 15 minutes to cool to a warm temperature.

3 Remove the star anise and serve in bowls with Greek yoghurt.

Brioche frangipane apple pudding

When you feel in need of a comfort pudding this one really fits the bill. It's perfect for Sunday lunch, served warm with ice cream, custard, cream or crème fraîche.

SERVES 8

½ brioche loaf
175g (6oz) butter, softened,
   plus extra for greasing
175g (6oz) caster sugar
1 tsp almond extract
175g (6oz) ground almonds
3 eggs, beaten
25g (1oz) plain flour
About 2 red dessert apples, skin
   on, cored and thinly sliced,
2 tbsp apricot jam
1 tbsp flaked almonds, toasted
Icing sugar, for dusting

PREPARE AHEAD
Can be made and baked up to
8 hours ahead and reheated to serve.

1 You will need a large, shallow ovenproof dish, about 28cm (11in) in diameter. Preheat the oven to 200°C/180°C fan/Gas 6 and grease the dish with butter.

2 Slice the brioche into thin slices, about 5mm/¼in, and arrange these over the base of the dish. Make sure you cover the base and fill in all the gaps, but don't overlap the slices.

3 Measure the butter and sugar into a food processor and whizz until pale and fluffy. Add the almond extract, ground almonds, eggs and flour, then whizz again until the mixture is soft and creamy and there are no lumps. Be careful not to over-process.

4 Spoon the mixture over the brioche base and spread it to the sides. Arrange the sliced apples in a neat overlapping circular pattern over the top. Bake the pudding in the oven for about 40 minutes until lightly golden all over and firm in the centre when lightly pressed.

5 Melt the jam with 2 tablespoons of water in a small pan. Brush over the surface and sprinkle with flaked almonds.

6 Dust the pudding with icing sugar and serve warm.

Bread & butter pudding with pecan maple topping

This pudding has been around forever and there have been many different variations over the years. Recipes often include spice, but I have removed the spice and added a lovely nutty glaze instead. It's best to use a wide dish, rather than a deep one.

SERVES 6

100g (4oz) caster sugar
100g (4oz) sultanas
Grated zest of 1 lemon
3 eggs
150ml (5fl oz) pouring double
    cream
300ml (10fl oz) milk
8 thin slices of white bread
75g (3oz) butter, melted, plus
    extra for greasing

FOR THE TOPPING
25g (1oz) pecan nuts, coarsely
    chopped
3 tbsp maple syrup

PREPARE AHEAD
*Can be assembled ready for baking
up to 4 hours ahead.*

1 You will need a wide 2–2.25-litre (3½–4 pint) ovenproof dish. Preheat the oven to 200°C/180°C fan/Gas 6 and grease the dish with butter.

2 Measure the sugar, sultanas and lemon zest into a bowl. In a separate bowl, mix the eggs, cream and milk and then pour into a large jug.

3 Lay the bread out on a board. Brush the slices with melted butter, then slice each piece into four triangles.

4 Arrange half the triangles over the base of the dish and scatter over the sultana mixture. Arrange the remaining triangles of bread over the top. Pour over the egg mixture and leave the pudding to stand for about an hour if you have time.

5 Bake in the oven for 30–40 minutes until the bread is golden and the custard is set in the middle.

6 Put the pecans in a small frying pan and toast for a few minutes until browned. Remove from the heat, add the maple syrup and stir. Immediately spoon the topping over the pudding and serve warm with pouring cream.

Toffee pear pudding

The ultimate comfort dessert – this is gooey and warming with a nice touch of freshness from the pear. As naughty as a pudding can be!

SERVES 6–8

1 x 400g (14oz) tin of pear
  halves, drained and dried
75g (3oz) butter, softened,
  plus extra for greasing
150g (5oz) light muscovado
  sugar
2 large eggs
175g (6oz) self-raising flour
1 tsp bicarbonate of soda
2 tbsp black treacle
125ml (4½fl oz) milk

FOR THE SAUCE
100g (4oz) butter
175g (6oz) light muscovado
  sugar
400ml (14fl oz) double cream
½ tsp vanilla extract
2 tbsp black treacle

PREPARE AHEAD
Can be made and cooked,
without the sauce, up to 6 hours
ahead. Sauce can be made up to
2 days ahead.

1 You will need a shallow 2-litre (3½-pint) ovenproof dish, measuring about 30 x 20 x 6cm (12 x 8 x 2½in). Preheat the oven to 180°C/160°C fan/Gas 4 and lightly grease the dish with butter.

2 Slice one pear half into thin horseshoe shapes and set these aside for decoration. Cut the remaining pears into 1cm (½in) pieces.

3 To make the pudding, measure the butter and sugar into a mixing bowl. Using an electric hand whisk, beat until light and creamy. Add the remaining ingredients and whisk again to make a smooth, thick batter. Stir in the chopped pears.

4 Pour into the prepared dish. Bake in the oven for about 40 minutes until the pudding is well risen, coming away from the sides of the dish and springy to the touch.

5 To make the sauce, measure all the ingredients into a saucepan and heat gently until the butter has melted. Increase the heat and boil for a couple of minutes, stirring all the time until the sauce has thickened slightly.

6 Arrange the reserved pear slices along the centre of the dish. Pour half the sauce over the pudding, then pour the rest into a warm jug. Serve the pudding warm, with the sauce and some ice cream, custard or cream.

Chocolate steamed pudding with chocolate sauce

Rich and indulgent, this is such a comforting pudding. There's nothing tricky or clever, just a lovely light sponge that's rich in flavour and served with a divine pouring sauce.

SERVES 6–8

125g (4½oz) baking spread, plus extra for greasing
125g (4½oz) caster sugar
2 large eggs
100g (4oz) self-raising flour
25g (1oz) cocoa powder, sifted
1 tsp vanilla extract

CHOCOLATE SAUCE
150ml (5fl oz) milk
150ml (5fl oz) double cream
300g (11oz) Bournville chocolate, broken into pieces
1 tsp vanilla extract

PREPARE AHEAD
Can be made up to 4 hours ahead but don't turn it out – keep it warm in hot water. Sauce can be made up to a day ahead and reheated to serve.

1 You will need a 1.1-litre (2-pint) pudding basin. Grease it with baking spread, then cut a small square of baking paper (about the size of the base of the bowl), grease it and place in the base of the basin, pressing it into the corners.

2 Measure all the pudding ingredients into a mixing bowl. Whisk with an electric hand whisk until well blended, light and fluffy. Spoon the mixture into the basin and level the top.

3 Cut a square of foil about 4cm (1½in) bigger than the top rim of the pudding and grease the underside with butter. Make a pleat in the middle of the square. Place it on top of the basin and tightly press around the edges, then tie with string to seal.

4 Put a small plate or a trivet in the base of a deep saucepan. Place the basin on top and pour in enough boiling water to come halfway up the sides and cover with a lid. Bring the water back to the boil, then reduce the heat and simmer very gently for 1½–1¾ hours until firm to touch on top when gently pressed.

5 To make the chocolate sauce, measure the milk and cream into a saucepan. Heat until just boiling, then add the chocolate and vanilla. Remove the pan from the heat and stir until the chocolate has melted.

6 Carefully remove the basin from the pan and take off the foil. To turn out, loosen around the edges with a knife, then turn upside down on to a plate and remove the bowl. Remove the paper on top. Pour some warm sauce over the pudding and cut into wedges. Serve the remaining sauce in a jug.

Apple & blackberry crumble

The most classic of comfort food puddings, this crumble is simple to make and perfect for an autumn day when apples and blackberries are in season. Expect the fruit juices to ooze around the edges and seep a little into the topping – this is all part of a crumble's charm.

SERVES 6

700g (1lb 7oz) Bramley apples, peeled and thickly sliced
600g (1lb 5oz) fresh blackberries
75g (3oz) caster sugar

FOR THE CRUMBLE TOPPING
175g (6oz) plain flour
50g (2oz) semolina
50g (2oz) light brown muscovado sugar
100g (4oz) butter, cubed
25g (1oz) demerara sugar, for sprinkling

PREPARE AHEAD
Can be assembled up to 6 hours ahead.

FREEZE
Freezes well assembled but unbaked.

1 You will need a shallow 1.75-litre (3-pint) ovenproof dish. Preheat the oven to 200°C/180°C fan/Gas 6.

2 Measure the apples, blackberries and sugar into the dish. Using a spoon, toss to coat the fruit in the sugar.

3 Measure the topping ingredients, except the demerara sugar, into a food processor. Whizz for a few moments until the mixture resembles breadcrumbs. Alternatively, rub the flour, semolina and muscovado sugar into the butter with your fingertips.

4 Scatter the crumble mixture evenly over the fruits and sprinkle the demerara sugar on top. Bake for about 45–50 minutes until pale golden brown on top and bubbling around the edges. Serve with custard, cream or ice cream.

Rustic apple tart

Unfussy, simple, comforting and delicious, this tart can be made in moments!

SERVES 6

350g (12oz) Bramley apples,
    peeled and diced
100g (4oz) caster sugar
Plain flour, for dusting
500g (1lb 2oz) block of
    all-butter puff pastry
1 egg, beaten
2 Braeburn apples, skin on,
    very thinly sliced
2 tbsp demerara sugar
3 tbsp apricot jam

PREPARE AHEAD
*Can be assembled up to the addition
of the apple purée up to 4 hours
ahead. Arrange the sliced apples
on top just before cooking.*

1 You will need a large baking sheet lined with baking paper. Preheat the oven to 220°c/200°c fan/Gas 7.

2 Put the Bramley apples, caster sugar and a tablespoon of water into a saucepan and stir over the heat for a few minutes until the sugar has dissolved. Cover the pan with a lid and simmer gently for about 10 minutes until the apples are soft. Increase the heat and cook to drive off any excess liquid, then mash the apples to a smooth purée. Leave to cool.

3 Lightly dust a work surface with flour and roll the pastry out to a circle roughly 25cm (10in) in diameter. Transfer to the baking sheet and brush the border of the circle with beaten egg. Fold in the edges and twist. To do this, push down on the edge of the pastry with your finger and twist the pastry over.

4 Spread the apple purée in the middle of the circle. Arrange the sliced apples around the edge of the tart and a few in the middle to make a pretty pattern. Sprinkle with the demerara sugar and brush the pastry with more beaten egg.

5 Bake in the oven for 30–35 minutes until well risen and lightly golden on top and brown and crisp underneath.

6 Melt the apricot jam in a saucepan until runny. Brush the tart with the glaze and serve warm with crème fraîche.

Real pouring custard

Some of the fresh custards available to buy are very good, but proper homemade custard is a real treat. Luxurious and silky, it is well worth making in my opinion.

MAKES 700ML (1¼ PINTS)

600ml (1 pint) full-fat milk
150ml (5fl oz) double cream
50g (2oz) caster sugar
2 tbsp cornflour
4 egg yolks
1 scant tbsp vanilla extract

PREPARE AHEAD
Can be prepared ahead of time,
then reheated gently, while stirring,
in a non-stick pan.

1 Warm the milk and cream in a saucepan until just simmering.

2 Measure the caster sugar, cornflour, egg yolks and vanilla extract into a mixing bowl and whisk together. Pour over the hot milk and cream and whisk quickly until smooth. Rinse out the saucepan, then pour the custard mixture through a sieve into the clean pan.

3 Heat over a medium heat, whisking all the time until the custard has thickened. Be careful not to let it boil. Remove the pan from the heat and pour the custard into a jug to serve.

Bakes

Bakewell tart fingers

I have happy memories of making these with my children when they were young.
Bakewell is often made as a round tart, but it is just as easy to make as fingers.

MAKES 16 FINGERS

FOR THE PASTRY
175g (6oz) plain flour
100g (4oz) butter
2 tbsp icing sugar, plus
    extra for dusting
1 egg, beaten

FOR THE FILLING
100g (4oz) butter, softened
100g (4oz) caster sugar
2 large eggs
100g (4oz) ground almonds
1 tbsp plain flour
1 tsp almond extract
½ jar of good raspberry jam
25g (1oz) flaked almonds

PREPARE AHEAD
Can be made up to 2 days ahead.

FREEZE
Freezes well once cooked.

1   You will need a 33 x 23cm (13 x 9in) Swiss roll tin. Preheat the oven to 200°c/180°c fan/Gas 6.

2   For the pastry, measure the flour, butter and sugar into a food processor and whizz until the mixture looks like breadcrumbs. Add the beaten egg and whizz until the pastry comes together. Alternatively, rub the flour, butter and sugar together in a bowl with your fingertips before adding the egg. Roll the pastry out very thinly, then use it to line the base and sides of the tin. Prick the base, then chill in the fridge or freezer for about 30 minutes.

3   Line the pastry with non-stick baking paper and baking beans. Bake blind for about 15 minutes, then remove the paper and beans and bake for another 5 minutes until the pastry is pale golden.

4   For the frangipane filling, measure the butter and sugar into the food processor. Whizz until creamy, then add the eggs and whizz again. Lastly add the ground almonds, flour and almond extract, then whizz.

5   Spread the jam over the base of the tart. Spoon the frangipane in blobs on top and spread it out to make an even layer. Sprinkle with flaked almonds. Put back into the oven for 18–20 minutes until lightly golden and set on top. Leave to cool, then slice into 16 fingers. Dust with icing sugar to serve.

Lemon shortbread with raspberries & cream

A lovely light shortbread, these are sandwiched with raspberries
and lemon cream for a teatime treat.

MAKES 10 SHORTBREAD
SANDWICHES

FOR THE LEMON SHORTBREAD
150g (5oz) butter, softened,
    plus extra for greasing
150g (5oz) plain flour
50g (2oz) semolina
50g (2oz) caster sugar
Zest of 1 small lemon
Icing sugar, for dusting

FOR THE FILLING
200ml (7fl oz) double cream
200g (7oz) Greek yoghurt
2 tbsp lemon curd
300g (11oz) raspberries

PREPARE AHEAD
*Can be assembled up to 2 hours
before serving and kept in the fridge.*

FREEZE
Cooked shortbread freezes well.

1 You will need a 23 x 33cm (9 x 13in) Swiss roll tin. Preheat
   the oven to 180°C/160°C fan/Gas 4. Lightly grease the tin
   with butter.

2 Measure the butter, flour, semolina, sugar and lemon zest into
   a food processor. Whizz until the mixture comes together and
   nearly forms a dough. Tip the mixture into the tin and use the
   back of a spoon to spread it out evenly to make a thin level layer
   across the base.

3 Bake for about 15–20 minutes until pale golden and firm in the
   middle. Leave to cool for 5 minutes, then score into 20 rectangles.
   Carefully remove them using a small palette knife and leave to
   cool on a wire rack.

4 Whisk the cream until it forms soft peaks, then stir in the
   yoghurt and lemon curd.

5 Spread one side of each piece of shortbread with lemon cream.
   Top half of them with raspberries, then sit another piece of
   shortbread, cream side down, on to the raspberries. Dust with
   icing sugar and serve at room temperature.

Cranberry, orange & pistachio biscuits

These biscuits are dancing with flavour. They keep well for up to a month – just layer them with kitchen paper in a sealed container to prevent them from softening.

MAKES 20

100g (4oz) butter, softened

75g (3oz) caster sugar, plus extra for dusting

1 egg yolk

1 tbsp milk

200g (7oz) plain flour, plus extra for dusting

Finely grated zest of 1 small orange

50g (2oz) dried cranberries, chopped

25g (1oz) shelled pistachio nuts, finely chopped

PREPARE AHEAD
Can be made up to a day ahead.

FREEZE
These freeze well.

1 You will need 2 baking sheets lined with baking paper and a 7cm (3in) fluted pastry cutter. Preheat the oven to 200°c/ 180°c fan/Gas 6.

2 Measure the butter and sugar into a mixing bowl. Using an electric hand whisk, whisk until creamy and fluffy. Add the egg yolk, milk, flour and zest and whisk until the mixture comes together. Add the cranberries and nuts and gently knead the dough together.

3 Roll out the dough to ½cm (¼in) thick on a floured work surface. Cut out biscuits using the fluted cutter and place them on the baking sheets, leaving a gap between each one. Re-roll the dough until you have 20 biscuits and all the dough is used.

4 Bake the biscuits for about 15 minutes until pale golden on top and underneath. Dust with caster sugar and transfer to a wire rack to cool.

Orange shortbread fingers

As some of you may know, shortbread is my absolute favourite biscuit.
These go well with any mousse or fool but are particularly good with the
Wild Bramble Mousse on page 227.

MAKES 36

100g (4oz) semolina
100g (4oz) caster sugar
225g (8oz) plain flour
225g (8oz) butter, cubed,
  plus extra for greasing
Finely grated zest of 1 small
  orange
25g (1oz) demerara sugar

PREPARE AHEAD
*Can be made up to a week ahead
and kept in an airtight container.
Put baking paper between the layers.*

FREEZE
These freeze well cooked.

1 You will need a small shallow tin, like a Swiss roll tin, 23 x 33cm
   (9 x 13in). Preheat the oven to 180°C/160°C fan/Gas 4. Lightly
   grease the tin with butter.

2 Measure the semolina, sugar, plain flour, butter and orange zest
   into a food processor. Whizz until the mixture comes together
   into a ball of dough.

3 Tip into the prepared tin and, using the back of a spoon, push
   the dough into the tin to make it an even thickness. Smooth the
   surface with the spoon, then chill for about 30 minutes.

4 Sprinkle with the demerara sugar and bake for about 25–30
   minutes until pale golden. Leave to cool slightly in the tin, then
   cut into 36 thin fingers – 3 across the short side of the tin and
   12 along the long edge. Using a palette knife, carefully transfer
   them to a wire rack to cool completely.

Tiny chocolate cupcakes

Made in mini-muffin tins, sometimes called mini cupcake tins, these adorable
little cakes are perfect for children – they will love the chocolate topping! If you only
have one tin, make the cakes in three batches.

MAKES 36 MINI CAKES

1 tbsp cocoa powder, sieved
2 tbsp boiling water
2 large eggs
100g (4oz) baking spread
100g (4oz) caster sugar
100g (4oz) self-raising flour
1 tsp vanilla extract

FOR THE ICING
100g (4oz) chocolate spread

PREPARE AHEAD
Can be made up to a day ahead.

FREEZE
*Freeze well – ice on the day
of serving.*

1   You will need 3 x 12-hole mini-muffin tins, lined with petit four
    cases. Preheat the oven to 180°c/160°c fan/Gas 4.

2   Measure the cocoa powder and boiling water into a large bowl.
    Mix until the cocoa has dissolved and the mixture is runny.
    Add the remaining ingredients and whisk with an electric hand
    whisk until light and fluffy in texture. Spoon into the cases.

3   Bake for about 12–15 minutes until the cakes are well risen and
    spring back when pressed lightly with a finger. Leave to cool in
    their paper cases on a wire rack.

4   Spread a little chocolate spread over the top of each cake.

Chocolate & strawberry dessert cake

Perfect for a celebration, this is a decadent dessert cake – one to be eaten with
a fork! Like a roulade, it contains no flour, which means it is a rich close-textured
sponge, so expect it to dip a little when it comes out of the oven.

SERVES 8–10

Butter, for greasing
6 eggs, separated
150g (5oz) caster sugar
50g (2oz) cocoa powder, sieved

FOR THE FILLING & TOPPING
300ml (10fl oz) double cream
2 tbsp icing sugar
1 tsp vanilla extract
400g (14oz) strawberries, sliced
   (reserve 3 whole strawberries)
Rosemary sprigs or mint leaves

PREPARE AHEAD
*Cakes can be made up to a day
ahead and assembled and filled
up to 2 hours ahead.*

FREEZE
*Cakes, without cream and fruit,
freeze well.*

1   You will need two 20cm (8in) round, loose-bottomed sandwich
    tins. Preheat the oven to 180°c/160°c fan/Gas 4, then grease
    the tins and line the bases with baking paper.

2   Put the egg whites into a bowl and whisk with an electric hand
    whisk until soft peaks form and the whites are fluffy and look
    like clouds. Spoon into a separate bowl.

3   Put the yolks and caster sugar into the unwashed main bowl.
    Whisk with an electric hand whisk until thick and there is a trail
    in the mixture when the whisk is lifted. Carefully fold the whites
    into the yolk mixture, then fold in the cocoa, a little at a time,
    until well mixed. Divide the mixture evenly between the prepared
    tins and level the tops.

4   Bake in the oven for about 25 minutes until the cakes are well
    risen and coming away from the sides of the tins. Turn out and
    leave to cool on a wire rack.

5   Whisk the cream into soft peaks, then stir in the icing sugar and
    vanilla extract. Spread half the cream over one cake and arrange
    half the strawberries on top. Put the second cake on top and
    spread with the rest of the cream.

6   Place the remaining strawberries in a pretty arrangement on top
    of the cake, with a few whole strawberries and rosemary sprigs
    or mint leaves in the middle. Dust with icing sugar just before
    serving and cut into slices.

Chocolate yoghurt cake

We have always liked cakes made with yoghurt, as it gives a lovely dense texture.
This is not a light cake but more like a Madeira.

SERVES 8

75g (3oz) baking spread
200g (7oz) Greek yoghurt
300g (11oz) caster sugar
175g (6oz) self-raising flour
50g (2oz) cocoa powder, sieved
3 large eggs
1 level tsp baking powder
2 tbsp milk

FOR THE CHOCOLATE
BUTTER ICING
225g (8oz) butter, softened
300g (11oz) icing sugar, plus
   extra for dusting
2 tbsp milk
3 tbsp cocoa powder, sifted

PREPARE AHEAD
*Can be made and assembled
up to 8 hours ahead.*

FREEZE
*The cooked sponges freeze well,
but it is always best to ice the cake
on the day of serving.*

1 You will need two 20cm (8in) sandwich tins. Preheat the oven to 180°C/160°C fan/Gas 4, then grease the tins and line each base with a circle of baking paper.

2 Measure all the cake ingredients into a bowl and whisk with an electric hand whisk until light and fluffy. Divide the mixture evenly between the prepared tins and level the tops.

3 Bake for about 25–30 minutes until the cakes are golden and shrinking away from the tins. The tops should spring back when pressed lightly with a finger. Leave to cool in the tins for about 10 minutes, then run a blunt knife around the edges to free the sponges. Turn the cakes out and leave to cool completely on a wire rack. Peel off the baking paper.

4 Measure the icing ingredients into a food processor and whizz for a minute until combined and smooth. Be careful not to over whizz or the icing will be grainy.

5 Sit one cake on a plate and spread with half the icing, taking it evenly to the edges. Sit the other cake on top and swirl the remaining icing on top to make a pretty pattern. Dust with icing sugar and cut into wedges to serve.

Coffee & hazelnut praline cake

Indulgent, sweet, impressive and comforting! This is definitely a special occasion cake – not one for everyday.

SERVES 6–8

1 tbsp coffee granules
1 tbsp just-boiled water
4 eggs
225g (8oz) baking spread,
  plus extra for greasing
225g (8oz) caster sugar
225g (8oz) self-raising flour
1 tsp baking powder

FOR THE PRALINE
100g (4oz) granulated sugar
75g (3oz) whole hazelnuts

FOR THE BUTTERCREAM
ICING
1½ tbsp coffee granules
1½ tbsp just-boiled water
225g (8oz) butter, softened
400g (14oz) icing sugar

PREPARE AHEAD
Can be assembled and iced up to a day ahead and decorated with the praline up to 8 hours before serving.

FREEZE
The cake, without icing, freezes well.

1 You will need two 20cm (8in) round, loose-bottomed sandwich tins and a baking sheet lined with non-stick baking paper. Preheat the oven to 180°C/160°C fan/Gas 4, then grease the tins and line each base with a disc of baking paper.

2 Dissolve the coffee granules in the hot water and stir until smooth. Measure the eggs, baking spread, sugar, flour and baking powder into a large mixing bowl and add the dissolved coffee mix. Beat with an electric hand whisk until well mixed and no lumps of fat remain. Divide between the tins and level the tops.

3 Bake in the oven for about 30 minutes until well risen and just shrinking away from the sides of the tins. Leave to cool slightly, then remove from the tins and leave to cool on a wire rack.

4 For the praline, measure the sugar and 4 tablespoons of water into a saucepan. Stir slowly over a low heat until the sugar has dissolved and you have a clear syrup. Remove the spoon and stop stirring, then increase the heat and boil until the syrup is pale golden. Add the hazelnuts and swirl the syrup in the pan to coat them, then quickly tip the mixture on to the lined baking sheet. Leave to cool and harden into a praline. Break the praline up on a wooden board and chop into very small pieces.

5 For the buttercream icing, dissolve the coffee in the hot water and stir until smooth. Measure the butter into a large bowl. Beat until smooth with an electric hand whisk, then add the coffee mixture and the sugar, a little at a time, and beat until smooth, light and fluffy.

6 Sit one cake on a plate. Spread with half the icing and sprinkle with half the praline. Sit the second cake on top and spread with the remaining icing, then sprinkle over the rest of praline. Cut into slices to serve.

Granny's gingerbread

This delicious cake is old-fashioned and so moreish – when we were testing this recipe, we couldn't eat it fast enough! The raw mixture is a batter, rather than a thick cake mix. The cake is beautifully sticky but light in texture and not too dense. My grandchildren love it!

MAKES 24 PIECES

225g (8oz) self-raising flour
1 tsp bicarbonate of soda
2 tbsp ground ginger
1 tsp mixed spice
100g (4oz) butter, diced
100g (4oz) black treacle
100g (4oz) golden syrup
100g (4oz) light muscovado sugar
1 egg, beaten
275ml (9fl oz) full-fat milk

PREPARE AHEAD
Can be made a day ahead.

FREEZE
Freezes well.

1   You will need a 23 x 30cm (9 x 12in) traybake tin lined with baking paper. Preheat the oven to 180°C/160°C fan/Gas 4.

2   Measure the flour, bicarbonate, ginger and mixed spice into a large bowl.

3   Measure the butter, treacle, syrup and sugar into a small saucepan and heat gently until the butter has just melted. Set aside to cool a little.

4   Pour the mixture from the saucepan into the bowl of dry ingredients. Add the beaten egg and beat with a wooden spoon until combined. Gradually add the milk, beating to make a smooth batter.

5   Pour the batter into the prepared tin and bake for about 35 minutes or until dark golden and springy to the touch. Cut into 24 pieces to serve. Wrapped tightly, this keeps for up to a week.

Passion fruit lemon cake

This is a simple sponge to make but, with its three tiers and luxurious filling, it is impressive. You can buy passion fruit curd, but it is sold more in delis than in supermarkets, so I've used lemon curd. Choose purple bobbly passion fruit, as they are ripe and have more pulp than the completely smooth, pale ones. And drizzling the passion fruit over the cream, rather than mixing it in, gives a more intense flavour. If the juice runs down the sides of the cake, even better!

SERVES 8

4 eggs
225g (8oz) baking spread, plus extra for greasing
225g (8oz) self-raising flour
225g (8oz) caster sugar
1 tsp baking powder
Finely grated zest of 1 small lemon

FOR THE TOPPING
450ml (15fl oz) double cream
4 passion fruit
4 tbsp lemon curd

PREPARE AHEAD
Sponges can be made up to a day ahead. Can be assembled up to 4 hours ahead and kept in the fridge.

FREEZE
Sponges freeze well.

1 You will need three 20cm (8in) loose-bottomed sandwich tins. Preheat the oven to 180°C/160°C fan/Gas 4. Grease the bases of the tins and line with baking paper.

2 Measure all the cake ingredients into a large bowl. Whisk, using an electric hand whisk, until well mixed and light and fluffy. Spoon the batter into the tins and level the tops. Bake for about 25 minutes until the cakes are coming away from the sides of the tins and they are risen and lightly golden. Leave to cool on a wire rack.

3 Whisk the double cream to soft peaks. Cut 3 of the passion fruit in half, scoop out the pulp into a bowl and set aside.

4 Spread the top of each cake with lemon curd. Sit one cake on a plate and spoon on a third of the cream, then spread it to the edges. Drizzle half the passion fruit pulp on top of the cream. Place a second cake on top and repeat, then add the third cake and finish with the remaining cream. Swirl the top with the back of a knife to make a pretty pattern. Slice the remaining passion fruit into wedges and arrange on top. Serve the cake at room temperature, cut into slices.

Tea loaf with cranberries & sultanas

I love an old-fashioned tea loaf. Spread with real unsalted butter and served with tea in bone china cups as I sit by the fire with our spaniels stretched out on the rug, it's my idea of heaven.

MAKES 1 LOAF

175g (6oz) dried cranberries
175g (6oz) sultanas
300ml (10fl oz) strong
  Earl Grey tea
Butter, for greasing
275g (10oz) self-raising flour
225g (8oz) light muscovado
  sugar
1 large egg, beaten

PREPARE AHEAD
Can be made up to 2 days ahead.

FREEZE
Freezes well.

1 Measure the dried fruits and tea into a bowl, then stir and cover the bowl with cling film. Leave to soak overnight or until all the liquid has been absorbed into the fruit.

2 You will need a 900g (2lb) loaf tin. Preheat the oven to 160°C/140°C fan/Gas 3. Grease the tin with butter and line it with baking paper.

3 Add the flour, sugar and egg to the bowl of fruit and mix well with a wooden spoon. Spoon the mixture into the loaf tin and level the top. Bake in the oven for about 1 hour and 40 minutes, until pale golden and firm to touch.

4 Run a palette knife round the edge of the loaf, then leave to cool slightly. Remove from the tin and place on a wire rack to cool completely. To serve, slice and spread with butter.

Irish soda bread

Soda bread is one of the quickest breads to make, as it has bicarbonate of soda as a raising agent instead of yeast. The buttermilk reacts with the soda to form bubbles and start the rising process, but this is still a denser loaf than bread made with yeast.

MAKES 1 ROUND LOAF

150g (5oz) plain white flour, plus extra for dusting

350g (12oz) plain wholemeal flour

1 tbsp runny honey

1 tsp salt

2 tsp bicarbonate of soda

1 x 284ml (10fl oz) carton of buttermilk

6 tbsp milk

1 Line a baking sheet with non-stick baking paper and dust it with flour. Preheat the oven to 220°c/200°c fan/Gas 7.

2 Measure the flours, honey, salt and bicarbonate into a large mixing bowl. Add the buttermilk and milk and bring the mixture together with a knife.

3 Tip the mixture on to a board and gently knead into a dough, being careful not to overwork it. Shape into a flat round loaf, measuring about 20cm (8in) wide, and place on the baking sheet. Score the top with a small cross, cutting about halfway through the dough.

4 Bake in the oven for about 20–25 minutes or until the bread is golden and well risen. It should sound hollow when the base of the loaf is tapped.

5 Place on a wire rack, cover with a tea towel and leave to cool before slicing.

Focaccia with olives, tomatoes & rosemary

Bread is a natural comfort food. As a nation we eat slightly less of it now, so it is such a treat to make your own bread that's full of flavour and texture. Be careful not to have the water too hot or it will kill the yeast and the bread won't rise.

MAKE 1 FOCACCIA

450g (1lb) strong white bread flour, plus extra for dusting

1 x 7g (¼oz) packet of fast-action dried yeast

1 tbsp olive oil, plus extra for greasing

½ tsp salt

1 tsp caster sugar

300ml (10fl oz) warm water

1 egg, beaten

Sea salt

FOR THE FLAVOURINGS

150g (5oz) olives, roughly chopped

100g (4oz) sun-dried tomatoes, roughly chopped

100g (4oz) Parmesan cheese, finely grated

2 garlic cloves, crushed

1 sprig of rosemary

PREPARE AHEAD
Can be made up to a day ahead but best made fresh on the day.

FREEZE
Freezes well once cooked.

1 You will need a 23 x 33cm (9 x 13in) Swiss roll tin. Preheat the oven to 220°C/200°C fan/Gas 7. Lightly grease the tin with oil.

2 To make the dough, measure the flour, yeast, oil, salt, sugar and water into a free-standing food mixer. Using the dough hook, switch the machine on to medium speed until you have a smooth dough (about 5 minutes). Alternatively, mix in a bowl and knead by hand for 10–15 minutes.

3 Grease a large bowl with oil. Add the dough, cover with cling film, and leave to rise in a warm place for about 1–1½ hours or until doubled in size.

4 Tip the dough on to a floured board. Knead for 3–4 minutes, and then add the olives, tomatoes, cheese and garlic. Knead together until everything is incorporated.

5 Push the dough out into the tin. Snip the rosemary into little sprigs and insert them into the dough, arranging them evenly over the top. Place the tin in a clean plastic bag and leave to prove in a warm place for about 30 minutes until light and puffy. Brush with beaten egg and sprinkle with sea salt.

6 Bake for 25–30 minutes until well risen and golden brown on top and underneath. Slice and serve with olive oil and balsamic vinegar for dipping.

Mary's Kitchen Guidance

Advice on freezing

The freezer is an essential in a modern kitchen, and it would certainly have been difficult for me to cope with feeding a family or entertaining if I could not have prepared a number of recipes in advance, freezing them until needed. I also hate waste, so instead of leaving leftovers in the fridge hoping they will be used up quickly, I try to freeze them. The trick to using your freezer wisely is to keep a note of everything you have in there. I keep mine as a list stuck on the inside of my kitchen cupboard. Look at your list before you make a meal and cross items off when they have been eaten.

WHAT YOU CAN FREEZE

MAIN COURSES

I find it invaluable to freeze meals for supper or dinner parties, and will often double up a recipe to make one dish for supper and one for another time. Most cooked dishes are best frozen for no longer than 3 months so they retain their original flavour.

VEGETABLES

They do taste better fresh, but vegetables can be a useful thing to have in the freezer. Most vegetables need to be blanched before freezing as this helps to retain their colour, texture, flavour and the vitamins within them. Plunge them into boiling water and cook for 1–3 minutes, then immediately drain and plunge into ice-cold water. Certain watery vegetables, such as cucumber, endives, lettuce, radishes and artichokes, cannot be frozen. Tomatoes can be frozen but are only suitable to add to casseroles as they become very watery.

FRUIT

Most freeze well and make an excellent stand-by dessert. Apples, rhubarb, plums, peaches, cherries and gooseberries are best stewed with a little sugar. Soft fruits such as strawberries or peaches are best turned into purées, as the whole frozen fruit will turn mushy when you defrost them. Smaller fruits like raspberries, blackberries, blackcurrants and redcurrants can be frozen whole.

CAKES AND PUDDINGS

Anything with delicate icing or decoration (such as piped cupcakes) should be open frozen so that it is not damaged when wrapped or packaged. To open freeze, spread the items out on a tray and place in the freezer. When they are completely frozen, they can be packed in containers or bags without damaging the shape.

BISCUIT AND PASTRY DOUGH

Biscuit dough can be frozen in a log shape, ready to be defrosted in the fridge, then sliced and baked. Pastry cases can be frozen unbaked or baked blind ready to fill. Uncooked pastry freezes perfectly for up to 3 months.

MILK, CREAM AND BUTTER

It is useful to keep milk in the freezer, as if you run out, it can be easily defrosted in a sink of cold water. The milk and fat will separate, but will homogenise again when shaken. Single cream and yoghurt do not freeze, but double and clotted cream can be frozen as they have a higher fat content. Freeze cream for up to 3 months only. Butter and hard cheese (ideally grated so it is ready to use) are also useful to keep in the freezer – again for only 3 months. Buttercream icing does freeze well, but use after 3 months or the flavour will deteriorate.

EGGS

Whole eggs do not freeze well, so do not add them to a fish pie if you are freezing it. Egg whites can be frozen in small containers (make sure you label how many you have frozen) and are ideal for meringues. Egg yolks can also be frozen in small containers to enrich sauces or omelettes at a later date.

WINE

Wine can be frozen in ice cube trays ready to add to sauces. When frozen, decant into small bags to store.

JARS OF SAUCES

If you have half a jar of any pasta sauce, roasted red peppers or pesto left over, decant into containers and freeze. Passata and chopped tomatoes also freeze well if you have some spare.

DO NOT FREEZE

RAW MEAT AND FISH THAT HAS BEEN FROZEN

To prevent the quality from deteriorating, it is always best not to refreeze anything that has been frozen previously. However, if it is in perfect condition, it should be safe when defrosted thoroughly.

PAVLOVA AND MERINGUE

Cooked meringue or pavlova will keep well in an airtight container, so there is no need to freeze them. Store in a cool place for up to 2 months.

SALAD INGREDIENTS

Ingredients like cucumber and lettuce contain too much water to freeze well, and would turn mushy once defrosted.

FRESH BASIL, CORIANDER AND DILL

It is better to make herbs into pesto or herb butters and freeze those instead.

POTATOES

If you are making a cottage pie or fish pie with mashed potato, add less milk and more butter to the potato or it will become watery when defrosted.

GENERAL FREEZER GUIDANCE

- For food safety reasons, cool foods completely after cooking or blanching before freezing.

- Exclude as much air as possible from packaged foods to prevent them drying out, and use the correct-sized container if possible.

- Keep washed cartons from ready-made foods. I wash out and keep ice cream and soup cartons that have tight-fitting lids, as these are so useful for freezing portions of food.

- Double wrap foods in foil first, then in waxed paper or a freezer bag. This will help prevent them from being damaged while frozen.

- Always date and label the packages, and add cooking/reheating instructions too.

- Organise the shelves. Try to keep the same sorts of foods together in sections of your freezer. For example, keep vegetables in one drawer, desserts and cakes in another and so on. Try to keep a good rotation of stock, using up the oldest foods first. Keep all the small ingredients that will easily get lost in one area of the freezer (e.g. chillies, sausages, fresh herbs, cubes of stock or wine).

DEFROSTING

- For best results, always defrost foods in the fridge, otherwise use the defrost setting on the microwave.

- You can defrost casseroles or soups on the hob but stir thoroughly during defrosting to ensure they're heated through evenly.

- Meat, fish and poultry must reach boiling point for 10 minutes in the centre (3–4 minutes in the microwave) to ensure they are cooked thoroughly.

- Most vegetables can be cooked from frozen.

- Some meals can be cooked from frozen: follow any specific guidance in the recipe, but generally increase the cooking time in the recipe by half again and ensure the centre of the food has reached boiling point for at least 10 minutes before serving.

- If defrosting in the microwave, ensure food is of even thickness or it will cook unevenly.

Conversions & measurements

MEASUREMENTS

METRIC	IMPERIAL
5mm	¼in
1cm	½in
2.5cm	1in
5cm	2in
7.5cm	3in
10cm	4in
12.5cm	5in
15cm	6in
18cm	7in
20cm	8in
23cm	9in
25cm	10in
30cm	12in

OVEN TEMPERATURES

°C	FAN °C	°F	GAS MARK
140°C	Fan 120°C	275°F	Gas 1
150°C	Fan 130°C	300°F	Gas 2
160°C	Fan 140°C	325°F	Gas 3
180°C	Fan 160°C	350°F	Gas 4
190°C	Fan 170°C	375°F	Gas 5
200°C	Fan 180°C	400°F	Gas 6
220°C	Fan 200°C	425°F	Gas 7
230°C	Fan 210°C	450°F	Gas 8
240°C	Fan 220°C	475°F	Gas 9

VOLUME

METRIC	IMPERIAL
25ml	1fl oz
50ml	2fl oz
85ml	3fl oz
100ml	3½fl oz
150ml	5fl oz (¼ pint)
200ml	7fl oz
300ml	10fl oz (½ pint)
450ml	15fl oz (¾ pint)
600ml	1 pint
700ml	1¼ pints
900ml	1½ pints
1 litre	1¾ pints
1.2 litres	2 pints
1.25 litres	2¼ pints
1.5 litres	2½ pints
1.6 litres	2¾ pints
1.75 litres	3 pints
1.8 litres	3¼ pints
2 litres	3½ pints
2.1 litres	3¾ pints
2.25 litres	4 pints
2.75 litres	5 pints
3.4 litres	6 pints
3.9 litres	7 pints
4.5 litres	8 pints (1 gallon)

WEIGHTS

METRIC	IMPERIAL
15g	½oz
25g	1oz
40g	1½oz
50g	2oz
75g	3oz
100g	4oz
150g	5oz
175g	6oz
200g	7oz
225g	8oz
250g	9oz
275g	10oz
350g	12oz
375g	13oz
400g	14oz
425g	15oz
450g	1lb
550g	1¼lb
675g	1½lb
750g	1¾lb
900g	2lb
1.5kg	3lb
1.75kg	4lb
2.25kg	5lb

Quantities

Over the years, I have been fortunate enough to have given many large parties at home and in the garden, and I have learned that the more people you have, the less they seem to eat! Most people cook far more than they need to, and I always feel that it is a shame to be so wasteful. Below is a rough quantities calculator that I use to work out recipes for my events. Of course, quantities will vary slightly depending on your guests, the time of day and the type of party you are hosting.

SAVOURY DISHES (PER PERSON)

Joint with bone: 175-225g (6-8oz)

Joint without bone: 100-175g (4-6oz)

Meat for casseroles: 175g (6oz)

Pasta, uncooked: 75-100g (3-4oz)

Rice, uncooked: 40-50g (1½-2oz)

Salmon: 100-125g (4-4½oz)

Soup: 600ml (1 pint) will serve 3 people

Fillet steak: 150g (5oz)

Other steaks: 175-200g (6-7 oz)

SWEET DISHES (PER PERSON)

Cakes: a 20cm (8in) sponge will feed 6

Meringues: 1 egg white and 50g (2oz) caster sugar will make about 5 small meringues

Soft fruits: 75-100g (3-4oz)

Cream to accompany desserts: 600ml (1 pint) per 12 portions

NIBBLES (PER PERSON)

Crisps: 25g (1oz)

Salted nuts: 15g (½oz)

BREAD AND SANDWICHES

1 loaf, medium cut, makes 10 rounds of sandwiches

100g (4oz) butter is enough for 1 large sandwich loaf or 12 bread rolls

1 long baguette can be cut into 20 slices

DRINKS

Champagne: 1 bottle (75cl) will serve 6 full glasses (8 if pouring smaller measures)

Wine: 1 bottle (75cl) will serve 6 glasses

Soft drinks and mixers: 1 bottle (1 litre) will serve 6 glasses

Milk for coffee: allow 900ml (1½ pints) per 20 cups

Milk for tea: allow 600ml (1 pint) per 20 cups

Index

A

almonds: Bakewell tart fingers 256
brioche frangipane apple
pudding 240
anchovies: rustic smoked trout &
anchovy pâté 33
apples: apple & blackberry
crumble 248
brioche frangipane apple
pudding 240
pork en croute with Stilton &
apple 124
rustic apple tart 250
Swedish meatballs with enriched
apple & thyme sauce 114
warming autumn fruit
compote 238
artichokes: onion, artichoke & sage
open tart 166
asparagus: hot smoked salmon &
asparagus salad 87
mild curried chicken with grapes
& asparagus 55
penne pasta with peppers, garlic
mushrooms & asparagus 159
posh bacon, asparagus &
mushroom spaghetti 121
aubergines: French slow-roast lamb
with ratatouille 144
orzo salad with grilled vegetables
& olives 156
avocados: hot smoked salmon &
asparagus salad 87
Mexican chicken & avocado
sharing platter 59
open chicken, bacon & avocado
sandwich 64
warm chicken Caesar, bacon &
avocado wraps 62

B

bacon: boeuf Bourguignon 138
open chicken, bacon & avocado
sandwich 64
posh bacon, asparagus &
mushroom spaghetti 121
posh jacket potatoes 172
sausage & red pepper hot pot 117
spinach frittata quiche 34
stir-fried chicken & vegetable
rice 68
warm chicken Caesar, bacon &
avocado wraps 62
Bakewell tart fingers 256
basil: basil & garlic dressing 212
pesto 172
Thai basil & lime sauce 99
beans: braised lamb with sweet
potato & haricot beans 143
Mexican chilli con carne 135
mixed bean & butternut wraps 171
smoky beef casserole with black-
eyed beans 130
veggie burgers 152
Béarnaise sauce 132
beef: boeuf Bourguignon 138
Bolognese bake 128
cottage pie with a bit of a kick 136
matchday beef & ale shortcrust
pie 140
Mexican chilli con carne 135
mustard steak with vine
tomatoes 132
smoky beef casserole with black-
eyed beans 130
beer: matchday beef & ale
shortcrust pie 140
beetroot: golden roasted
vegetables 204
pickled beetroot 202
rosy-pink beetroot, feta & olive
salad 215
biscuits: cranberry, orange &
pistachio biscuits 260

freezing 285
orange shortbread fingers 263
black-eyed beans, smoky beef
casserole with 130
blackberries: apple & blackberry
crumble 248
warming autumn fruit
compote 238
wild bramble mousse 227
blinis, crab & herb 84
Bloody Mary dressing 42
blueberries: lemon & blueberry
mousse with hazelnut & oat
topping 228
warming autumn fruit
compote 238
boeuf Bourguignon 138
Bolognese bake 128
bread: croque Monsieur 41
focaccia with olives, tomatoes &
rosemary 281
Irish soda bread 278
open chicken, bacon & avocado
sandwich 64
bread & butter pudding with pecan
maple topping 242
brioche frangipane apple
pudding 240
broad beans, roasted pepper &
tomato salad with 212
broccoli: cauliflower, broccoli & leek
Mornay 175
Emerald Isle garden soup 29
roasted pepper, mushroom &
broccoli brown rice salad 216
burgers, veggie 152
burrata with heritage tomato
salad 42
butter: buttercream icing 270
caper butter 100
chilli garlic butter 196
chocolate butter icing 268

foolproof Béarnaise sauce 132
freezing 285–6
garlic butter 88
tarragon butter 50
butterbeans: veggie burgers 152
buttermilk: Irish soda bread 278
butternut squash: golden roasted
vegetables 204
marigold soup 22
mixed bean & butternut wraps 171
split roasted butternut squash
with chilli garlic butter 196
squash & parsnip roasties 182
super veg with brown rice &
herbs 178

C

cabbage: colcannon mash 189
stir-fried aromatic Hispi
cabbage 209
cakes: chocolate & strawberry
dessert cake 267
chocolate yoghurt cake 268
coffee & hazelnut praline cake 270
freezing 285
Granny's gingerbread 273
passion fruit lemon cake 274
tea loaf with cranberries &
sultanas 276
tiny chocolate cupcakes 264
capers: caper butter 100
caper herb dip 105
caramel: coffee & hazelnut praline
cake 270
toffee pear pudding 245
carrots: carrot & swede purée 198
marigold soup 22
cauliflower: cauliflower, broccoli &
leek Mornay 175
golden cauliflower steaks with
tomato & garlic salsa 163
golden roasted vegetables 204
paneer & roasted vegetable
curry 168
roasting tin Thai salmon &
vegetables 92

salmon fillets with cauliflower
cheese topping 102
celebration trifle 220
cheese: Bolognese bake 128
burrata with heritage tomato
salad 42
cauliflower, broccoli & leek
Mornay 175
croque Monsieur 41
double-baked mushroom
soufflés 30
feta & olive tapenade 210
focaccia with olives, tomatoes &
rosemary 281
leek & dill quiche 176
mac 'n' cheese 154
mustard Parmesan dressing 72
onion, artichoke & sage open
tart 166
paneer & roasted vegetable
curry 168
penne pasta with peppers, garlic
mushrooms & asparagus 159
pesto 172
pork en croute with Stilton &
apple 124
rosy-pink beetroot, feta & olive
salad 215
salmon fillets with cauliflower
cheese topping 102
spinach frittata quiche 34
stuffed portabella mushrooms
with Brie & spinach 36
sweet potato & spinach
pithivier 164
see also **goat's cheese**
cheesecake, divine white chocolate
chilled 224
cherries: Irish Cream & cherry
pots 231
chicken: chicken & fennel fricassee
with tarragon 70
chicken hot pot with potato
topping 52
five-spiced chicken with coriander
& cucumber relish 56

Mexican chicken & avocado
sharing platter 59
mild curried chicken with grapes
& asparagus 55
open chicken, bacon & avocado
sandwich 64
preserved lemon chicken 48
roast chicken with tarragon butter
& melting onions 50
smoky firecracker chicken
drumsticks 67
Sri Lanka chicken curry 60
stir-fried chicken & vegetable
rice 68
warm chicken & dill salad 72
warm chicken Caesar, bacon &
avocado wraps 62
warming chicken noodle soup 24
chickpeas: pea & mint dip 38
chillies: chilli garlic butter 196
crab linguine 82
five-spiced chicken with coriander
& cucumber relish 56
Mexican chilli con carne 135
chocolate: chocolate & raspberry
layered pots 232
chocolate & strawberry dessert
cake 267
chocolate steamed pudding with
chocolate sauce 246
chocolate yoghurt cake 268
decadent orange, chocolate &
whisky mousse 237
divine white chocolate chilled
cheesecake 224
Irish Cream & cherry pots 231
tiny chocolate cupcakes 264
cider, simmered red cabbage & 206
coconut milk: roasting tin Thai
salmon & vegetables 92
Sri Lanka chicken curry 60
cod: cod goujons with caper herb
dip 105
Thai cod cakes 99
coffee & hazelnut praline cake 270
colcannon mash 189

coriander: coriander & cucumber relish 56
crab linguine 82
fragrant lemongrass & coriander rice 184
spiced quail with coriander dressing 78
cottage pie with a bit of a kick 136
courgettes: Emerald Isle garden soup 29
grilled garlic prawns & Mediterranean vegetables 88
roasting tin Thai salmon & vegetables 92
super veg with brown rice & herbs 178
crab: crab & herb blinis with pickled fennel herb salad 84
crab linguine 82
crackling 122
cranberries: cranberry, orange & pistachio biscuits 260
tea loaf with cranberries & sultanas 276
cream: bread & butter pudding with pecan maple topping 242
celebration trifle 220
chocolate & raspberry layered pots 232
chocolate & strawberry dessert cake 267
decadent orange, chocolate & whisky mousse 237
freezing 285–6
Irish Cream & cherry pots 231
lemon posset tart 222
lemon ripple ice cream 234
passion fruit lemon cake 274
real pouring custard 253
wild bramble mousse 227
see also soured cream
cream cheese: divine white chocolate chilled cheesecake 224
Irish Cream & cherry pots 231
crème fraîche: mustard Parmesan dressing 72

croque Monsieur 41
crumble, apple & blackberry 248
cucumber: coriander & cucumber relish 56
coriander dressing 78
cupcakes, tiny chocolate 264
curry: braised lamb with sweet potato & haricot beans 143
mild curried chicken with grapes & asparagus 55
paneer & roasted vegetable curry 168
Sri Lanka chicken curry 60
custard: celebration trifle 220
real pouring custard 253

D
decadent orange, chocolate & whisky mousse 237
defrosting 287
dill: warm chicken & dill salad 72
dips: caper herb dip 105
pea & mint dip 38
soured cream chive dip 194
divine white chocolate chilled cheesecake 224
dressings: basil & garlic dressing 212
Bloody Mary dressing 42
coriander dressing 78
fennel mustard dressing 87
hoisin dressing 75
lemon herb dressing 156
maple dressing 64
mustard Parmesan dressing 72
duck salad with hoisin dressing 75

E
eggs: freezing 286
glorious fish pie 106
hot smoked salmon & asparagus salad 87
spinach frittata quiche 34
toasted muffins with scrambled eggs & smoked salmon 44
Emerald Isle garden soup 29

F
fennel: chicken & fennel fricassee with tarragon 70
fennel mustard dressing 87
grilled garlic prawns & Mediterranean vegetables 88
pickled fennel herb salad 84
salmon & fennel one-pot wonder 94
super veg with brown rice & herbs 178
fish: glorious fish pie 106
see also cod, salmon etc
five-spiced chicken with coriander & cucumber relish 56
focaccia with olives, tomatoes & rosemary 281
fragrant lemongrass & coriander rice 184
frangipane: brioche frangipane apple pudding 240
freezing 285–7
French slow-roast lamb with ratatouille 144
fricassee, chicken & fennel 70
fries, sweet potato skinny 201
frittata: spinach frittata quiche 34
fruit: freezing 285
see also apples, raspberries etc

G
garlic: basil & garlic dressing 212
chilli garlic butter 196
garlic butter 88
rack of lamb with garlic minted potatoes 147
ridged garlic potatoes 186
gingerbread, Granny's 273
goat's cheese: posh jacket potatoes 172
golden cauliflower steaks 163
golden roasted vegetables 204
Granny's gingerbread 273
grapes: mild curried chicken with grapes & asparagus 55
gravy 50, 147

onion gravy 122
Greek salad with feta & olive tapenade 210

H
haddock: glorious fish pie 106
haddock & shrimp feast 96
ham: croque Monsieur 41
orange-glazed ham with mango & orange salsa 126
stuffed portabella mushrooms with Brie & spinach 36
haricot beans: braised lamb with sweet potato & haricot beans 143
harissa: harissa marinade 118
marinated harissa & yoghurt pork kebabs 118
hazelnuts: coffee & hazelnut praline cake 270
lemon & blueberry mousse with hazelnut & oat topping 228
herbs 286
see also **basil, dill** *etc*
hoisin dressing 75
hot pot: chicken hot pot with potato topping 52
sausage & red pepper hot pot 117

I
ice cream, lemon ripple 234
icing: buttercream icing 270
chocolate butter icing 268
chocolate icing 264
Irish Cream & cherry pots 231
Irish soda bread 278

K
kebabs, marinated harissa & yoghurt pork 118
kidney beans: Mexican chilli con carne 135
veggie burgers 152
kidneys, mustard 148

L
lamb: braised lamb with sweet

potato & haricot beans 143
French slow-roast lamb with ratatouille 144
rack of lamb with garlic minted potatoes 147
lasagne: baked pasta lasagne rolls 112
leeks: cauliflower, broccoli & leek Mornay 175
Emerald Isle garden soup 29
glorious fish pie 106
leek & dill quiche 176
mushroom & leek soup 26
pheasant & port stew 76
sweet potato & spinach pithivier 164
warming chicken noodle soup 24
lemon: lemon & blueberry mousse with hazelnut & oat topping 228
lemon herb dressing 156
lemon posset tart with fresh raspberries 222
lemon ripple ice cream 234
lemon shortbread with raspberries & cream 258
passion fruit lemon cake 274
preserved lemon chicken 48
lemongrass & coriander rice 184
lentils: mushroom, lentil & double potato jumble 160
lettuce: duck salad with hoisin dressing 75
rosy-pink beetroot, feta & olive salad 215
warm chicken Caesar 62
limes: crab linguine 82
hoisin dressing 75
Thai basil & lime sauce 99
linguine, crab 82

M
macaroni: mac 'n' cheese 154
mango & orange salsa 126
maple syrup: bread & butter pudding with pecan maple topping 242

maple dressing 64
marigold soup 22
marinades: harissa marinade 118
spiced marinade 78
matchday beef & ale shortcrust pie 140
mayonnaise: caper herb dip 105
meatballs, Swedish 114
Mexican chicken & avocado sharing platter 59
Mexican chilli con carne 135
milk: freezing 285–6
real pouring custard 253
mint: pea & mint dip 38
mixed bean & butternut wraps 171
mousses: decadent orange, chocolate & whisky mousse 237
lemon & blueberry mousse with hazelnut & oat topping 228
wild bramble mousse 227
muffins: toasted muffins with scrambled eggs & smoked salmon 44
mushrooms: baked pasta lasagne rolls 112
boeuf Bourguignon 138
Bolognese bake 128
chicken hot pot with potato topping 52
double-baked mushroom soufflés 30
haddock & shrimp feast 96
mushroom & leek soup 26
mushroom, lentil & double potato jumble 160
onion, artichoke & sage open tart 166
penne pasta with peppers, garlic mushrooms & asparagus 159
posh bacon, asparagus & mushroom spaghetti 121
posh jacket potatoes 172
roasted pepper, mushroom & broccoli brown rice salad 216
stir-fried chicken & vegetable rice 68
stuffed portabella mushrooms with Brie & spinach 36

super veg with brown rice &
    herbs 178
warming chicken noodle soup 24
mussels: seafood risotto 91
mustard: fennel mustard dressing 87
    mustard kidneys 148
    mustard Parmesan dressing 72
    mustard steak with vine
        tomatoes 132

N

noodles: warming chicken noodle
    soup 24

O

oats: lemon & blueberry mousse
    with hazelnut & oat topping 228
olives: feta & olive tapenade 210
    focaccia with olives, tomatoes &
        rosemary 281
    orzo salad with grilled vegetables &
        olives 156
    rosy-pink beetroot, feta & olive
        salad 215
onions: French slow-roast lamb with
    ratatouille 144
    onion, artichoke & sage open
        tart 166
    onion gravy 122
    roast chicken with tarragon butter
        & melting onions 50
    roasted pepper, mushroom &
        broccoli brown rice salad 216
    spiced quail with coriander
        dressing 78
    see also shallots; spring onions
oranges: cranberry, orange &
    pistachio biscuits 260
    decadent orange, chocolate &
        whisky mousse 237
    orange-glazed ham with mango &
        orange salsa 126
    orange shortbread fingers 263
orzo salad with grilled vegetables &
    olives 156

P

paneer & roasted vegetable curry 168
Parma ham: stuffed portabella
    mushrooms with Brie & spinach 36
parsnips: golden roasted
    vegetables 204
    squash & parsnip roasties 182
passion fruit lemon cake 274
pasta: baked pasta lasagne rolls 112
    Bolognese bake 128
    crab linguine 82
    mac 'n' cheese 154
    orzo salad with grilled vegetables
        & olives 156
    penne pasta with peppers, garlic
        mushrooms & asparagus 159
    posh bacon, asparagus &
        mushroom spaghetti 121
pastries: pork en croute with Stilton
    & apple 124
    spicy sausage rolls 110
    see also pies; tarts
pastry 176, 256
    freezing 285
    shortcrust pastry 140, 222
pâté, rustic smoked trout &
    anchovy 33
peas: Emerald Isle garden soup 29
    pea & mint dip 38
    salmon & fennel one-pot
        wonder 94
    seafood risotto 91
pears: celebration trifle 220
    toffee pear pudding 245
pecan nuts: bread & butter pudding
    with pecan maple topping 242
penne pasta with peppers, garlic
    mushrooms & asparagus 159
peppers: Emerald Isle garden soup 29
    French slow-roast lamb with
        ratatouille 144
    grilled garlic prawns &
        Mediterranean vegetables 88
    marinated harissa & yoghurt pork
        kebabs 118
    Mexican chicken & avocado

sharing platter 59
    Mexican chilli con carne 135
    orzo salad with grilled vegetables &
        olives 156
    penne pasta with peppers, garlic
        mushrooms & asparagus 159
    posh jacket potatoes 172
    roasted pepper & tomato salad
        with broad beans 212
    roasted pepper, mushroom &
        broccoli brown rice salad 216
    roasting tin Thai salmon &
        vegetables 92
    sausage & red pepper hot pot 117
    smoky beef casserole with black-
        eyed beans 130
    Sri Lanka chicken curry 60
    stir-fried chicken & vegetable
        rice 68
pesto: posh jacket potatoes 172
petits pois: Emerald Isle garden
    soup 29
    pea & mint dip 38
    salmon & fennel one-pot wonder 94
    seafood risotto 91
pheasant & port stew 76
pickles: pickled beetroot 202
    pickled fennel herb salad 84
pies: cottage pie with a bit of a
    kick 136
    matchday beef & ale shortcrust
        pie 140
    sweet potato & spinach
        pithivier 164
    see also pastries; tarts
pistachios: cranberry, orange &
    pistachio biscuits 260
pithivier, sweet potato & spinach 164
plums: warming autumn fruit
    compote 238
pork: marinated harissa & yoghurt
    pork kebabs 118
    pork en croute with Stilton &
        apple 124
    slow-roast hand & spring with
        crackling 122

Swedish meatballs with enriched
    apple & thyme sauce 114
port: cottage pie with a bit of a
    kick 136
    gravy 147
    pheasant & port stew 76
posh bacon, asparagus & mushroom
    spaghetti 121
posh jacket potatoes 172
posset: lemon posset tart 222
potatoes 286
    the best roast potatoes 190
    chicken hot pot with potato
        topping 52
    colcannon mash 189
    cottage pie with a bit of a kick 136
    glorious fish pie 106
    mushroom & leek soup 26
    mushroom, lentil & double potato
        jumble 160
    posh jacket potatoes 172
    potato wedges with soured cream
        chive dip 194
    rack of lamb with garlic minted
        potatoes 147
    ridged garlic potatoes 186
    sausage & red pepper hot pot 117
praline: coffee & hazelnut praline
    cake 270
prawns: grilled garlic prawns &
    Mediterranean vegetables 88
    seafood risotto 91
    see also **shrimp**

Q

quail: spiced quail with coriander
    dressing 78
quiches: leek & dill quiche 176
    spinach frittata quiche 34

R

raspberries: celebration trifle 220
    chocolate & raspberry layered
        pots 232
    lemon posset tart with fresh
        raspberries 222

lemon shortbread with raspberries
    & cream 258
raspberry jam: Bakewell tart
    fingers 256
ratatouille, French slow-roast lamb
    with 144
red cabbage: simmered red cabbage
    & cider 206
relish, coriander & cucumber 56
rice: fragrant lemongrass &
    coriander rice 184
    haddock & shrimp feast 96
    roasted pepper, mushroom &
        broccoli brown rice salad 216
    seafood risotto 91
    stir-fried chicken & vegetable
        rice 68
    super veg with brown rice &
        herbs 178
ridged garlic potatoes 186
risotto, seafood 91
rocket: roasted pepper & tomato
    salad with broad beans 212
rosy-pink beetroot, feta & olive
    salad 215
rustic apple tart 250
rustic smoked trout & anchovy
    pâté 33

S

sage: onion, artichoke & sage open
    tart 166
salads 286
    duck salad with hoisin dressing 75
    Greek salad with feta & olive
        tapenade 210
    hot smoked salmon & asparagus
        salad 87
    orzo salad with grilled vegetables
        & olives 156
    pickled fennel herb salad 84
    roasted pepper & tomato salad
        with broad beans 212
    roasted pepper, mushroom &
        broccoli brown rice salad 216
    rosy-pink beetroot, feta & olive

salad 215
    warm chicken & dill salad 72
salmon: roasting tin Thai salmon
    & vegetables 92
    salmon & fennel one-pot
        wonder 94
    salmon fillets with cauliflower
        cheese topping 102
salsas: avocado salsa 59
    mango & orange salsa 126
    tomato & garlic salsa 163
sandwiches: open chicken, bacon &
    avocado sandwich 64
sauces: cheese sauce 175
    chocolate sauce 246
    foolproof Béarnaise sauce 132
    freezing 286
    gravy 50, 147
    onion gravy 122
    real pouring custard 253
    Thai basil & lime sauce 99
    tomato sauce 112
sausage meat: baked pasta lasagne
    rolls 112
sausages: sausage & red pepper hot
    pot 117
    spicy sausage rolls 110
    seafood risotto 91
shallots: boeuf Bourguignon 138
shortbread: lemon shortbread 258
    orange shortbread fingers 263
shortcrust pastry 140, 222
shrimp: haddock & shrimp feast 96
    see also **prawns**
smoked haddock: glorious fish
    pie 106
smoked salmon: hot smoked salmon
    & asparagus salad 87
    toasted muffins with scrambled
        eggs & smoked salmon 44
smoked trout & anchovy pâté 33
smoky beef casserole with black-eyed
    beans 130
smoky firecracker chicken
    drumsticks 67
soda bread, Irish 278

soufflés, double-baked mushroom 30
soups: Emerald Isle garden soup 29
    marigold soup 22
    mushroom & leek soup 26
    warming chicken noodle soup 24
soured cream chive dip 194
spaghetti: posh bacon, asparagus &
    mushroom spaghetti 121
spinach: baked pasta lasagne
    rolls 112
    haddock & shrimp feast 96
    paneer & roasted vegetable
        curry 168
    spinach frittata quiche 34
    stuffed portabella mushrooms
        with Brie & spinach 36
    sweet potato & spinach
        pithivier 164
    veggie burgers 152
spring onions: colcannon mash 189
    crab linguine 82
    posh jacket potatoes 172
squash see butternut squash
Sri Lanka chicken curry 60
steak see beef
steamed pudding, chocolate 246
stews: boeuf Bourguignon 138
    braised lamb with sweet potato &
        haricot beans 143
    pheasant & port stew 76
    smoky beef casserole with black-
        eyed beans 130
    see also hot pot
stir-fries: aromatic Hispi
        cabbage 209
    chicken & vegetable rice 68
strawberries: chocolate & strawberry
    dessert cake 267
sultanas: bread & butter pudding
    with pecan maple topping 242
    tea loaf with cranberries &
        sultanas 276
super veg with brown rice &
    herbs 178
swede: carrot & swede purée 198
    marigold soup 22

Swedish meatballs with enriched
    apple & thyme sauce 114
sweet potatoes: braised lamb with
    sweet potato & haricot beans 143
    golden roasted vegetables 204
    mushroom, lentil & double potato
        jumble 160
    paneer & roasted vegetable
        curry 168
    sweet potato & spinach
        pithivier 164
    sweet potato skinny fries 201

T

tapenade, feta & olive 210
tarragon: chicken & fennel fricassee
    with tarragon 70
    tarragon butter 50
tarts: Bakewell tart fingers 256
    lemon posset tart with fresh
        raspberries 222
    onion, artichoke & sage open
        tart 166
    rustic apple tart 250
    see also pastries; pies; quiches
tea loaf with cranberries &
    sultanas 276
Thai cod cakes 99
tiger prawns: grilled garlic prawns &
    Mediterranean vegetables 88
    seafood risotto 91
tiny chocolate cupcakes 264
toffee pear pudding 245
tomatoes: Bloody Mary dressing 42
    Bolognese bake 128
    braised lamb with sweet potato &
        haricot beans 143
    burrata with heritage tomato
        salad 42
    focaccia with olives, tomatoes &
        rosemary 281
    French slow-roast lamb with
        ratatouille 144
    Greek salad with feta & olive
        tapenade 210
    Mexican chilli con carne 135

mustard steak with vine
    tomatoes 132
roasted pepper & tomato salad with
    broad beans 212
sausage & red pepper hot pot 117
smoky beef casserole with black-
    eyed beans 130
Sri Lanka chicken curry 60
tomato & garlic salsa 163
tomato sauce 112
veggie burgers 152
treacle: Granny's gingerbread 273
trifle, celebration 220
trout: smoked trout & anchovy
    pâté 33
    whole stuffed baked trout with
        caper butter 100

V

vegetables: freezing 285
    see also carrots, tomatoes etc
veggie burgers 152

W

warming autumn fruit compote 238
watermelon: duck salad with hoisin
    dressing 75
whisky: decadent orange, chocolate
    & whisky mousse 237
wild bramble mousse 227
wine: freezing 286
    gravy 50
wraps: Mexican chicken & avocado
    sharing platter 59
    mixed bean & butternut wraps 171
    warm chicken Caesar, bacon &
        avocado wraps 62

Y

yoghurt: chocolate yoghurt cake 268
    coriander dressing 78
    lemon & blueberry mousse 228
Yorkshire pudding 193

Thank you

Huge thank yous to so many from the bottom of my heart.

I am blessed to have the most talented, brilliant home team. It is here, in the kitchen, that all the creating, testing and tasting goes on till each recipe is as good as we can possibly make it.

Firstly, where would I be without Lucy Young, who has been by my side for 30 years? I do not make any decisions without her; she is wise, gentle and a tough perfectionist! Once we have decided on the recipes, Lucinda McCord starts testing them. It's always a team effort and Lucinda is wonderful at cracking on, using the expertise she has learnt with us over the last 20 years... We can't believe it is 20 years since she arrived straight from Leith's Cookery School!

Once the recipes are perfected, they are ready to be photographed for the book and TV. Lisa Harrison and Evie Harbury are the amazing home economist duo for the photography for this book and with lovely Isla Murray for the TV series. They are a hugely treasured part of our team. We have so much fun filming the series – thank you to Karen Ross and the fabulous team at Sidney Street, and it is a joy seeing the camera boys scrambling to take home some of the spoils.

The gorgeous recipe photographs have been taken by Laura Edwards. We are thrilled with the warmth and slightly more modern trend, and with Tabitha Hawkins's prop styling, which embraces the new trends of 2020, all very shabby chic in feel!

A big shout to BBC Books, who have done a fabulous job again. Lizzy Gray heads a great team and huge thanks to editor Charlotte Macdonald for all her meticulous care over the whole book. Thank you also to copy editor Jinny Johnson and Miranda Harvey our book designer. Also, big thanks to Georgia Glynn Smith for the lovely cover shot and forest photographs.

I'm always moaning that hair and makeup take too long, as I can't sit still, but the wonderfully talented Jo Penford is simply the best. Tess Wright guides me on clothes. I am very fussy, but Tess is wonderful at making me look OK.

Lastly my agents, Felicity Bryan and Joanna Kaye (KBJ), are always there with instant advice. They are my guardian angels, thank you. And to you all for buying the books and supporting me over the years.

BBC Books, an imprint of Ebury Publishing
20 Vauxhall Bridge Road,
London SW1V 2SA

BBC Books is part of the Penguin Random House group of companies whose addresses can
be found at global.penguinrandomhouse.com

This book is published to accompany the television series entitled *Mary Berry's
Simple Comforts,* first broadcast on BBC Two in 2020. *Mary Berry's Simple Comforts*
is a Sidney Street TV production.

BBC Commissioning Executive: Catherine Catton
Series Directors: Dave Crerar & Sarah Myland
Series Producer: Alice Binks
Director Of Photography: Rob Mansfield
Lighting Camera: Craig Harman & Lee Beavers
Lighting: Robin Johnson & Adam Carroll
Sound: Lloyd Williamson & Mike Stephenson
Home Economists: Lisa Harrison (lead) & Isla Murray
Art Director: Sophie Robinson
Production Managers: Bethany Medcalf (Snr) & Mary Mullarkey (Jnr)
Assistant Producers: Hannah Pereira & Ben Ibbott
Camera Assist: James Daly & Manuela Jaramillo
Runner: Alex Smith
Editors: Paul Clifton, Michelle Bromham, Steve Donlon & Chloe Walker
Edit Producers: Lucy Davis & Gina Mahoney
Executive Producer: Karen Ross

First published by BBC Books in 2020

www.penguin.co.uk

A CIP catalogue record for this book is available from the British Library

ISBN 9781785945076

Publishing Director: Lizzy Gray
Senior Editor: Charlotte Macdonald
Food Stylist: Lisa Harrison
Prop Stylist: Tabitha Hawkins
Design: Miranda Harvey
Testing: Isla Murray
Copy Editor: Jinny Johnson

Colour reproduction by Altaimage, London
Printed and bound in Germany by Mohn Media Mohndruck GmbH

Penguin Random House is committed to a sustainable future for our business, our readers and our
planet. This book is made from Forest Stewardship Council® certified paper.